The Church
of Notre-Dame
in Montreal

The Church of Notre-Dame in Montreal

An Architectural History

by Franklin Toker

McGill–Queen's University Press

Montreal and London   1970

© McGill-Queen's
University Press 1970
ISBN 0 7735 0058 8
Library of Congress
Catalog Card No. 70-98392
Designed by Robert R. Reid
Printed in Canada

*This work has been
published with the help
of a grant from the
Humanities Research
Council of Canada,
using funds provided
by the Canada Council,
and a grant in aid
of publication from
the Department of
Cultural Affairs of Quebec.*

To W. O. Judkins

Contents

List of Plates

Preface

$\mathfrak{I}$N WRITING about Notre-Dame de Montréal I have tried to set down the answers to questions which until now had not been asked regarding the building and renovation of the church. This method of questioning, which attempts to minimize the role of personal value judgements in architectural history, is parallel to what Reyner Banham calls "existential" or "situationist" criticism.* It is a relativistic criticism, based on the response of the architect to his problems and opportunities at every step during construction. In this case I have tried to use it to emphasize that the church of Notre-Dame is a work of art as well as a great and useful building. A possible disadvantage of situationist criticism, at least as I have used it, is the stress which it places on the architect to the detriment of the patrons and other groups who may have influenced the final design. It also places much greater emphasis on the original architect, James O'Donnell, than on Victor Bourgeau, although the latter was also responsible for the present attractiveness of Notre-Dame. I have attempted to balance this inequality by presenting the building of Notre-Dame as the creation of, or at least the result of, many complex forces which were at work in Quebec in the 1820's. Although it is no longer appropriate to regard Notre-Dame as the physical symbol of French Canada, as did Mgr. Olivier Maurault forty years ago, it is still important to understand why it was regarded so for over a century.

This study of Notre-Dame began on December 24, 1964, when the former

*Reyner Banham, "Convenient Benches and Handy Hooks: Functional Considerations in the Criticism of the Art of Architecture," in *The History, Theory and Criticism of Architecture*, pp. 91-105.

Preface Curé Jean-Baptiste Vinet, P.S.S., gave me a copy of Mgr. Maurault's *La Paroisse: Histoire de l'Eglise Notre-Dame de Montréal.* In the four years since then M. Vinet has granted me unrestricted freedom of access to the archives of his church and aided me with great patience and kindness. I have often taken advantage of the dedicated labour which the late Mgr. Maurault put into *La Paroisse* and of the fascinating study of attitudes which Professor Alan Gowans presented in his article "Notre-Dame de Montréal." Both authors kindly gave me further encouragement in private interviews.

Apart from particular debts which are acknowledged in the notes, I would like to express my thanks to the following persons who aided me in my research. In Ireland: His Excellency James A. Belton, Mrs. Eilish Ellis, The Honourable Desmond Guinness, Richard J. Hayes, Patrick Henchy, Myles McSwiney, and Patrick O'Donnell, Member of Parliament.

In England: H. M. Colvin, John Harris, and Sir John Summerson.

In Canada: Marie Baboyant, François Beaudin, Pierre-S. Beaudry, Pierre Beaulieu, John Bland, Paul Cholette, Edgar Andrew Collard, Antonio Dansereau, Jacques-H. Derome, J. Russell Harper, Harold Kalman, Hélène Lamy, Lawrence M. Lande, Jean-Jacques Lefebvre, Marguerite Mercier, Gérard Morisset, Mrs. John A. Morton, Elaine Poulin, Honorius Provost, Eric Reford, A. J. H. Richardson, Sister Miriam of the Temple, Monique Tessier, Jacqueline Trépanier, the late Léon Trépanier, Stanley Triggs, Charles de Volpi, and Louise Zunini. Special thanks are due to Armour Landry and Jeremy Taylor for their photographs, to Stefan Starenky for his drawings, and to Orson Wheeler, Special Lecturer in the Fine Arts at Sir George Williams University, for permission to illustrate his scale model of Notre-Dame.

In the United States: Mrs. C. L. Arnold, Betty Ezequelle, Mrs. Agnes Addison Gilchrist, Adolf Placzek, Mrs. Sarah E. Rusk, Richard Spear, John Spencer, and Helen Tanger.

My research outside the Archives of Notre-Dame was pursued mainly in the Salle Gagnon of the Bibliothèque de la Ville de Montréal; Séminaire de Saint-Sulpice and Bibliothèque Nationale, Montreal; Collection Baby, Bibliothèque de l'Université de Montréal; Archives de la Chancellerie de l'Archevêché de Montréal; l'Inventaire des Oeuvres d'Art du Québec and Archives du Séminaire de Québec in Quebec City; Avery Architectural Library, New York; Harvard College Library, Cambridge, Massachusetts; Geneology and Local History Room, New York Public Library; Library of the Maryland Historical Society, Baltimore; and Manuscript Division, Library of Congress, Washington.

The following have given permission to quote from their works: Professor Alan Gowans, for "The Baroque Revival in Québec," which appeared in the *Journal of the Society of Architectural Historians;* the Curé and Parish of

Notre-Dame, for the late Monseigneur Olivier Maurault's *La Paroisse;* M.
Gérard Morisset, for *L'Architecture en Nouvelle-France;* and The Macmillan
Company of Canada Limited, for the late Ramsay Traquair's *The Old
Architecture of Quebec.*

I have mentioned that this is a book of questions about Notre-Dame. It has
been my good fortune to study under John Coolidge, Professor of Fine Arts
at Harvard University, who encouraged me to rethink every concept I had
about Notre-Dame and to ask questions which had not occurred to me. For
his kindness and perception I am deeply grateful.

ᴠɪꜱɪᴛᴏʀꜱ ᴛᴏ ᴍᴏɴᴛʀᴇᴀʟ generally walk through the historic quarter of Old Montreal. There they find a variety of buildings ranging in style from Baroque to modern, crowded into a shallow rectangle of one hundred acres along the St. Lawrence River (*Plates* 1, 2). Although most of the architecture dates only from the nineteenth century, the whole district takes on an ancient air because of the uniform use of limestone. Erected side by side on narrow streets over a period of three hundred years, these warehouses, convents, and offices coalesce into three-story walls of grey stone. The layout of the streets, because it has scarcely changed since 1672, also makes this quarter distinctive. Encircled by protective walls until the early nineteenth century, the city could not expand; instead its buildings were packed more and more closely together. One striking reminder of the walls today is the winding of des Commissaires Street, which follows the jagged line of the old bastions.

The development of the old city had proceeded more in accordance with natural environment than with civic regulations. The lines of the original rectangle followed approximately the St. Lawrence River and La Petite Rivière (now Place d'Youville) on the east, the *ruisseau* Saint-Martin (Craig Street) on the west, a marsh (Place Victoria) on the south, and a natural bluff (Berri Street) on the north.* The land was very uneven, rising from sea level on the east to a peak of seventy-five feet just a fifth of a mile inland (Place d'Armes), then dropping to fifty feet at the western boundary (Craig Street). The lower level on the east was settled first because of proximity to the river for water

---

*Throughout this study, all directions are given according to points on the compass (*Plate* 2). Thus Notre-Dame Street is here said to run north-south, although in Montreal it is by convention considered to run east-west.

1

**Notre-Dame
de Montréal**

supply and transportation. But the annual floods of the St. Lawrence soon encouraged settlers to build along Saint-Paul Street, sixty feet above the water line, rather than closer to the river on what is now des Commissaires.

Montreal grew without planning from its founding in 1642 until 1672. By common usage the main north-south axis became Saint-Paul Street, parallel to the river and half-way up the hill. There were a number of east-west streets which intersected Saint-Paul, the principal one being Saint-Joseph. When the first ordinance controlling the streets was issued in 1672, all of the existing roads were retained despite their irregularity and narrowness. But there was enough empty land at the summit of the hill for the planners to lay out a new street, broad and perfectly straight from the north end of the settlement to the south. This important thoroughfare was named Notre-Dame in honour of the patron saint of Montreal. In the middle of the street, just south of its intersection with Saint-Joseph, the citizens immediately began to build a parish church, which they named Notre-Dame de Montréal. Their intention was to follow European precedent and lead Notre-Dame Street around the church in crescents on the east and west. Instead the priests designated a cemetery on the east side of the church, and traffic made a detour only on the west. When, in the early eighteenth century, this crescent-shaped detour had expanded into a trapezoid, it was given the grand but inappropriate name of Place d'Armes (*Plate* 4).

The Place d'Armes still exists and remains the site of the parish church of Notre-Dame. But the old Notre-Dame was replaced in 1829 by a newer church which stands to the east of its predecessor, on the site of the old cemetery (*Plate* 23). This church has a facade of dark grey limestone, 136 feet wide and 213 feet high. The smooth surface of its two square towers is broken by moldings which separate four pointed windows and an oculus. The central section of the front is only half as high as the towers. Pier buttresses and string courses subdivide it into six equal units: three below contain open pointed arches and three above form a blind arcade of niches. An embattled parapet crowns this portion of the facade.

Given no previous information, an acute observer could guess the approximate date of this facade. The neat grid of horizontal and vertical lines in the towers suggests an affinity with the eighteenth-century towers of Westminster Abbey. The smooth surface of the facade and the presence of Gothic elements used decoratively rather than structurally point to a kinship with pioneer experiments in the Gothic Revival in England and America in the early nineteenth century. Additionally, the visitor who has driven to Montreal through rural Quebec will recall seeing this type of flat stone facade with twin towers and three niches or windows over three doors in countless churches in the province, whether their decorative detail is Romanesque, Gothic, or Baroque.

Inside, the visitor discovers a vast space, broader and more restless than he would have imagined from the rather narrow and calm exterior (*Plate* 21). The volume of the interior suggest a kneading of space in the penetrations which slice boldly into the barrel vault over the nave and in the rhythm of spatial compartments formed by the ribbed vaults of the side aisles. The natural light which streams in through skylights in the ceiling and the rich colour and intricate carving of the columns bring out the surface texture of the nave. The nave may also be seen as a linear framework of strongly accented columns and gallery fronts, recalling the stone grid of the facade. The overall impression the visitor receives is that Notre-Dame is a theatre, provided with double galleries on three sides and a stage in the form of the shallow recess of the sanctuary. Dominating the nave is an illuminated reredos which rises seventy-five feet to the ceiling. Loaded with sculpture and ornament, the reredos acknowledges the influence of the Gothic Revival in France in the mid-nineteenth century. On the other hand, the broad proportions of the nave, the contour and low penetrations of the barrel vault, and the relation of the columns to the ceiling are found in English Georgian churches of the eighteenth century. Finally, as in the case of the exterior, similar features are found in hundreds of church interiors throughout the province of Quebec.

The architecture of this church presents certain problems. If one could isolate and identify the English, French, and American aspects of Notre-Dame, the analysis would still not account for their remarkable combination in this one building. The dissimilarity of nave and facade must also be explained. Going a step further, one would have to decide how the church could absorb so many sophisticated foreign elements and still have a kinship with the typical Quebec rural church. Without knowing the history of the church, its architects, and its dates, these problems cannot be unravelled. With such knowledge one can arrive at a partial answer, but the story of the building of Notre-Dame will appear no less unconventional.

T HE PRESENT CHURCH of Notre-Dame is a relative newcomer to Place d'Armes. Twice as old is the Séminaire de Saint-Sulpice, one hundred and twenty feet to the south (*Plate* 26). A three-story fieldstone building with a *corps de logis* of 1687 and projecting wings of the eighteenth and nineteenth centuries, the Seminary is the Canadian headquarters of the Messieurs de Saint-Sulpice. The Sulpicians, or Gentlemen of Saint-Sulpice, constitute a society of secular priests. They take no vows to the order, nor are they bound to remain in the community; they in effect live together to fulfil a common purpose of educating young men, primarily for the priesthood. The headquarters of the order are at Paris; their major American branches are at Baltimore and Washington.

The Sulpicians seldom seek or accept the administration of a parish church. Their relationship with Notre-Dame is unusual in that they not only officiate in the church, but also they use it as their equivalent of a monastic chapel. A large rectory serves as both a functional and a visual intermediary between the Seminary and the church, and it is in this neutral site that the Sulpicians act as parish priests when they consult with members of the congregation.

Not only the church of Notre-Dame, but also the entire city of Montreal owes its founding to the Sulpicians. Both the establishment of Montreal and the formation of the Sulpician order were conceived almost simultaneously in the mind of the seventeenth-century French theologian, Jean-Jacques Olier de Verneuil. In 1640 Olier became the principal supporter of La Compagnie de Notre-Dame de Mont-Réal.[1] His goal was the establishment of a Christian outpost among the Indians of the New World, complete with a school, a hospital, and a seminary. The logical place to send French missionaries was New

France. Within New France, a likely area to encounter Indians was the island of Mont-Réal in the St. Lawrence near the Ottawa River. In 1535 Jacques Cartier had visited the populous Mohawk village of Hochelaga on the island, but seventy-five years passed before the French tried to settle there. After Samuel de Champlain's abortive attempt in 1610, no further effort was made to colonize the island for thirty years.

In 1641 Louis XIII gave Olier's association the right to occupy Mont-Réal, and that same year thirty-five settlers were sent to New France. On February 27, 1642, Olier celebrated Mass in Notre-Dame de Paris and consecrated Mont-Réal to the Holy Family under the special protection of the Virgin Mary. Its name was then changed to Ville-Marie. On May 17, 1642, the colonists reached Ville-Marie from their winter shelter of Quebec. They built a wooden stockade by the water's edge at Pointe-à-Callières (approximately the corner of d'Youville and Saint-François-Xavier Streets today), south of the ruins of Champlain's trading post on Place Royale. Within this fort was the first wooden church of Notre-Dame. In 1644 Jeanne Mance chose a spot two hundred yards inland for the site of the Hôtel-Dieu hospital. This move established the first two streets of Montreal: the north-south path in front of the hospital became Saint-Paul Street, and the east-west path alongside became Saint-Joseph (today Saint-Sulpice). In 1659 the first church of Notre-Dame in the stockade was abandoned, and a new chapel was erected next to the hospital at the north-west corner of Saint-Paul and Saint-Joseph Streets. This second church, dedicated to the Virgin and to St. Joseph, patron of the hospital, was also built of wood but on a stone base. It was eighty feet long, thirty feet wide, and twenty feet high. On its roof was set a high steeple with a belfry and two bells.[2]

The growth of Montreal in its first decade was exceedingly slow. When Jeanne Mance visited France in 1649, she reported to Jean-Jacques Olier that the colony was in a state of near-collapse. However, since 1641 when his part in the establishment of Montreal had terminated, Olier had concentrated his immense energies on a second ambition: the formation of a seminary in which the sons of the aristocratic and intellectual élite of France could be trained for the priesthood. In December 1641 he established such a seminary at Vaugirand, near Paris. In 1642 Olier moved the seminary into the rectory of the parish of Saint-Sulpice in Paris. Under royal patronage, the Sulpicians erected a huge new church and seminary and began to extend their influence throughout Europe. Olier's two separate creations, Montreal and the Sulpician order, were to some extent amalgamated to meet the dire situation of Montreal in 1649. Olier first assumed the directorship of the Compagnie de Notre-Dame de Mont-Réal.[3] Next he sent four of the first graduates of his seminary to Montreal. These men, led by Gabriel de Queylus, arrived there in 1657 to

6

supplant the Jesuits who, until then, had been the spiritual leaders of Montreal. Consequently, the first and second parish churches of Montreal were not built under the patronage of the Sulpicians, although they did bring the second church to completion in 1659.

In 1663 a decisive change occurred in the administration of Ville-Marie. Through the intervention of their noble and royal supporters, the Paris Seminary of Saint-Sulpice was allowed by Louis XIV to buy the entire island of Montreal from its previous owners, the mercantile Compagnie des Cent-Associés. The Sulpicians also paid the debt incurred by the defunct Compagnie de Notre-Dame de Mont-Réal. Thus in 1663 the Sulpicians assumed the title of Seigneurs de Montréal and so held the island in the name of the King of France. They were obliged to administer justice, appoint the governor, defend the city, and provide such basic public services as a water supply and a system of roads.[4] In return the Sulpicians could extract four privileges from the inhabitants: the annual land tax of *cens et rentes* of six *deniers* per *arpent;* the eight per cent tax of *lods et ventes* whenever real estate changed hands; the rarely exercised obligation of free labour, called *corvée;* and the *banalité*, or fee for the compulsory use of the Seminary gristmills.[5] These rights were held by the Seminary of Montreal in the name of the Seminary of Paris until the British conquest of Montreal in 1760. Thereafter they were the legal privileges of the Canadian branch alone. Improbable though it seems, these feudal rights remained viable until the mid-nineteenth century. In 1819, for example, the Seminary successfully petitioned the British administration to destroy the gristmill of the banker John Fleming which threatened the Seminary monopoly.[6] In 1824 the seigniorial revenues amounted to £4,500 a year or £200 (perhaps equivalent to $6,000 today) per priest in the Seminary.[7]

Granting the seigniory of Montreal to the Sulpicians was almost certain to lead to conflict in New France. Montreal was one of the largest and certainly the richest seigniory in the colony, and one of the few owned outright by a religious community. Until 1663 the settlement at Montreal had vigorously competed with Quebec City for funds from the royal court. Now a religious dispute between the Sulpicians of Montreal and the Jesuits of Quebec exacerbated the political rivalry between the cities. In 1645 it seemed as though the first Bishop of New France would be installed at Montreal. Through alternate arrangements the first colonial bishop, Mgr. de Laval, resided instead at Quebec when he came over in 1659.[8] The Sulpicians thus constituted the supreme civil authority on the island of Montreal, but as priests they were subservient to the Bishop of Quebec.

Under capable and sometimes brilliant leadership Saint-Sulpice assumed greater spiritual authority as well. In 1664 the seminarians took possession of their permanent headquarters, a stone residence near Saint-Paul Street (destroyed by fire in 1850) in which the Governor seems to have resided as their guest.[9] They soon had to face their first challenge of spiritual authority from the Bishop of Quebec. In 1669 Mgr. de Laval called for the building of a new church commensurate with Montreal's population of almost one thousand. Land was immediately selected in the Lower Town, and funds and materials were pledged for the project. The Seminary, however, had already chosen an uptown site for their new residence and insisted that the new church be built adjacent to that site. They refused to contribute to the building of the new church, and the project soon collapsed.[10]

In 1666 the Sulpicians welcomed their most versatile member to Montreal: the soldier, historian, priest, and engineer François Dollier de Casson. De Casson served as Superior of the Seminary and consequently as seigneur of Montreal from 1671 to 1674 and again from 1678 to 1701. It was he who built the Montreal aqueduct and from 1689 to 1698 supervised the excavation of the *ruisseau* Saint-Martin in an attempt to create a canal around the St. Lawrence River rapids.[11]

De Casson, with the help of the city notary-surveyor Benigne Basset, tried to regularize the layout of the streets in 1672. He retained Saint-Joseph as the principal east-west axis from the docks up the hill and down to the bridge across the Saint-Martin. But he did not wish to keep Saint-Paul as the main north-south axis. Instead he laid out Notre-Dame Street on the summit of the hill. Besides being wide and straight, Notre-Dame joined the north and south gates and the two most important public utilities, the only windmill at the north end of town and the only public well on Place d'Armes.[12] The Seminary had chosen this spot for their new home and for the new parish church as well. On June 19, 1672, de Casson offered to build the inhabitants a new church in the middle of Notre-Dame Street, south of its intersection with Saint-Joseph. The next day he gave the land to the church corporation in his capacity as seigneur, and the following day he directed the digging of the foundation.[13] The church was to be approximately one hundred feet long and thirty feet wide.[14]

This third church of Notre-Dame, which was opened in 1683 and demolished in 1830, is only of peripheral interest to the history of the present fourth church.[15] Certain features, however, had a significant bearing on the construction of its successor. Perhaps the most important of these was its status. Although the Seminary had paid for the building of Notre-Dame and used it as a sort of monastic chapel, the church was administered at first by lay wardens. It was only in 1678 that by decree of the Bishop of Quebec, Notre-Dame became a parish church, united in perpetuity with the Seminary, and in 1694 the office of curé of Notre-Dame became an automatic function of the Superior of Saint-Sulpice.[16] At almost the same time the Seminary strengthened its political position with confirmation of its title to the seigniory in 1693 and again in 1714 by Louis XIV.[17]

As the symbolic centre of the increasing temporal and spiritual influence of the Sulpicians, the third church of Notre-Dame was enlarged several times and embellished with paintings, sculpture, and silver liturgical objects. The original shape of the church had been simply a rectangle. During the eighteenth century a transept, side aisles, a new facade, an imposing bell-tower, and a chain of sacristies were added to this nucleus (*Plate* 10). But the population of Montreal was also fast-expanding, and temporary expedients such as the addition of more galleries could not provide enough seating capacity. The wardens discussed rebuilding Notre-Dame as early as 1750 and 1757 and were earnestly exhorted to rebuild by Bishop Hubert of Quebec in 1789.[18] By the beginning of the nineteenth century the church was 125 years old and so inadequate that crowds had to stand outside the door to attend Mass.[19] In 1801 the church wardens decided that the old building would have to be abandoned; nevertheless in 1809 they obstinately refused to demolish the old church and instead had it redecorated and added a new facade.[20] This made the church more elegant but no larger (*Plate* 3). A plan for a completely new building was examined with favour in 1819, but once again the wardens chose not to destroy old Notre-Dame.[21] The church by this time had become a traffic nuisance because it blocked Notre-Dame Street at Place d'Armes. It remained the only parish church in a city of fifteen thousand Catholics, although its capacity did not exceed three thousand.

What can explain the reluctance of the wardens of Notre-Dame to build a new church? Apart from the natural factors such as lack of funds and a sentimental attachment to the old building, the probable motivation was the need to preserve the autonomy of the Séminaire de Saint-Sulpice. In fact, as it turned out, it was only a direct threat to that autonomy which precipitated the rebuilding of Notre-Dame with exceptional speed. The autonomy of the Sulpicians had been greatly strengthened by the British conquest of New France in 1759-60. First, their property rights and some seigniorial privileges were renewed by the British in part in 1781 and in full in 1841. For a time the Sulpicians were almost indispensable to the British in the orderly administration of the island. Second, the British had forced the extinction by 1800 of the Jesuits and Récollets (a branch of the Franciscans) in Quebec, leaving the Sulpicians as the only male religious order in the colony.[22] Moreover, the suppression of the mother house of the Sulpicians in Paris by the French Revolutionary Assembly in 1792 had brought to Montreal more than twenty of the most sophisticated and brilliant priests ever to serve in Canada, revitalizing the Montreal Seminary for a generation. The rise in influence of the Sulpicians was matched by the rise in influence of their church of Notre-Dame. In 1760 Montreal possessed five Catholic churches and chapels for public worship; in 1820 only three. The Jesuit church had been deconsecrated in 1789 and destroyed in 1810,[23] while the Chapelle de Sainte-Anne of 1693 had fallen into ruin.[24] The Récollet church and the old Chapel of Notre-Dame de Bon-Secours had been taken over by Notre-Dame as auxiliary chapels. That left Notre-Dame as the sole independent Catholic church in Montreal.

Notre-Dame was never more than a parish church, but through the power of the Sulpicians and the loss of the other churches, it had assumed the prestige of a cathedral. Its curé vowed allegiance not to the Bishop of Quebec but to the Superior-General of the Sulpician Seminary in Paris, which had been re-established under Napoleon in 1802. Further protection was afforded by the British administration which generally favoured the Seminary of Montreal over the Bishop of Quebec. Under the circumstances, one can imagine the reluctance of the Sulpicians and the wardens of Notre-Dame to lower the status of their church by constructing more churches in Montreal or by replacing the venerable monument with a modern structure. Rather than destroying old Notre-Dame, they encased it like a jewel in a new setting.

The autonomy of the Seminary ended abruptly in 1821, when one of its own members was appointed vicar-general of the district of Montreal and auxiliary to the Bishop of Quebec. The diocese of Quebec in 1783 had included all Canada as well as the east coast of North America from New Orleans to Labrador. The United States was detached from this giant diocese in the following decades but, in 1808, when Joseph-Octave Plessis became bishop, it still included all the British colonies in North America. Plessis sought permission from Rome to establish five new and independent dioceses: Nova Scotia, New Brunswick, Upper Canada (Ontario), the North-West Territories, and the city of Montreal. These purely religious affairs had to be approved by the Colonial Secretary in London before they could be effected by the Vatican. The Colonial Secretary approved the creation of the three English-speaking dioceses by 1819, but denied permission for separate dioceses of the North-West and Montreal because these districts were populated by French Canadians. It was considered desirable to keep to a minimum the number of clerical leaders among the French.[25] In 1819 Plessis travelled to London and to Rome to petition in person for the detachment of the two French-speaking districts. He took along as his assistant Jean-Jacques Lartigue, secretary of the Seminary of Montreal, who wanted to plead for the full restoration of the Sulpician property rights before the Colonial Secretary, Lord Bathurst.[26] Far from being a plot to cripple the power of the Seminary, the voyage of Bishop Plessis was intended to aid it, for Plessis himself argued persuasively for the restoration of these rights.[27] The Seminary was prepared to accept the creation of a bishopric of Montreal, provided that the bishop be a Sulpician, presumably Lartigue, and that the diocese of Montreal be entirely detached from the control of Quebec.[28]

Arrangements did not turn out quite as expected. London agreed only to allow auxiliary bishops to be appointed over Montreal and the territories of the North-West, as suffragans to the Bishop of Quebec.[29] Returning to Canada, Plessis consecrated Lartigue as his auxiliary for Montreal with the title of Mgr. de Telmesse on January 21, 1821. Significantly, the ceremony took place in the church of Notre-Dame itself.[30] The aspirations of the Sulpicians of almost two centuries had been fulfilled: an episcopal throne stood on the dais of Notre-Dame de Montréal. But to the unabated bitterness of the Sulpicians, this throne also represented the new control of the Bishop of Quebec over their affairs in Montreal.

The first victim of the Sulpician counter-attack was the offending episcopal throne. It was jettisoned from Notre-Dame by order of the wardens just one month after it was placed there by Plessis.[31] The Bishop of Quebec immediately wrote Lartigue:

> They have sent me a long memorandum to prove by demonstrative reason that all the honours that I vouchsafe to you, and to which you lay claim, are improper. I will not contest with its author but I shall send to Rome my pastoral letter of the twentieth of February and submit it to the judgement of the Holy See. In the meantime, do not dispute with them, but take the initiative. If they harass you, withdraw. In the absence of a throne, content yourself with a *prie-dieu;* if that is not to be had, seat yourself on the end of a bench, or what would be better still, cease to worship in a parish church which is no more a cathedral than any other church in the city; and adopt the church of the Hôtel-Dieu or any other.[32]

The Sulpicians struck out not only at Lartigue but at his superior Mgr. Plessis as well. In what was probably the most scurrilous attack in the history of the Church in Canada, the Seminary claimed at the Congregation of the Propagation of the Faith in Rome that Bishop Plessis had helped the British to sequester the Jesuit property in Canada in return for £1000 and a seat on the Legislative Council, and that he was now attempting to destroy the Sulpicians as well.[33]

Even Bishop Plessis admitted that his protégé Lartigue was too weak to put up much defence against the onslaught of the Sulpicians.[34] But other Montrealers came to the aid of the new auxiliary bishop. Lartigue was related through his mother to two powerful patrician dynasties in Montreal, the Papineau and Viger families. Neither family had served as wardens of Notre-Dame since the very early years of the nineteenth century. Whatever the cause of their conflict with the Sulpicians, subsequent events showed that these families were willing to make considerable sacrifices to further the cause of Lartigue.

Now two more old issues were brought into the attack on Saint-Sulpice: one social and political, the other racial. Since the British conquest, the population of Montreal had expanded outside the walls to occupy an area of about one thousand acres, compared to the original one hundred acres. In 1825 the population of the old quarter numbered five thousand and the population of the seven new suburbs, twenty thousand.[35] But until Montreal was incorporated as a city in 1832, the residents of the old city were distinctly favoured over those living in the suburbs. The thirty-two magistrates who governed the district of Montreal were selected proponderantly from the old area. The two-thirds of the Montrealers who were Catholics had extra cause for complaint. Many had to travel miles to attend Mass in Notre-Dame, which was held in the heart of the old city. Since the suburbs contained five times more Catholics than did the old city and had a much higher percentage of Catholics to Protestants, the establishment of a new church in the suburbs became extremely vital. As it happened, the Papineau and Viger families (led by the future mayor Jacques Viger) took part in this struggle on behalf of the suburbs. On September 25, 1822, over eleven hundred Catholics signed a petition to the Bishop of Quebec and Lartigue demanding a new church which would serve as the cathedral of Montreal and as the parish church for the western suburbs. About 95 per cent of the signatories were residents of the suburbs.

The racial issue was understandably less clear-cut. Until 1760 Montreal was an exclusively French-speaking, Catholic city. After the conquest English and Scottish settlers arrived in modest numbers, followed by many more Tories who moved north after the American Revolution. This immigration caused a certain degree of racial and religious antagonism, heightened by the Anglo-Scottish take-over from the French Canadians of the lucrative fur trade. But it was the war of 1812 that really brought prosperity to Montreal and induced a stream of immigration which threatened to turn the city into a French relic like present-day New Orleans.

The 1820's began as a disastrous decade for the French-speaking community of Montreal. In 1821 McGill was founded as the only university in the colony in a rather blatant attempt to Anglicize and Anglicanize young French Canadians. In 1822 a Bill of Union was proposed which would envelop French-speaking Lower Canada into the more populous English Upper Canada. English and Scottish immigrants came in unprecedented numbers, while Irish Catholic immigration had scarcely begun. In 1825 the whole city contained eighteen thousand Catholics and eight thousand non-Catholics, and the gap was narrowing rapidly. Ironically, the Sulpicians' excellent relations with the British changed with the new situation from an asset to a liability. The French-speaking community, looking to its leaders for support in countering the threat of the English, could not soon forget those who had celebrated Masses in Notre-Dame for the English victories over Napoleon, who had contributed so munificently to the local monument to Lord Nelson, and who had rallied the people so zealously to the cause of the British in the war of 1812.

The building of a Catholic cathedral in Montreal would not solve all of these religious, racial, and demographic problems, but it seemed an appropriate step to take. Supported by Bishop Plessis and certain leading families of Montreal, the new church of Saint-Jacques, named for the patron saint of Lartigue, was quickly planned and executed. It was the first new Catholic church to be built in the city in half a century. Denis-Benjamin Viger, Lartigue's cousin, donated the land in the midst of farms on Saint-Denis Street, west of the old city, and Louis-Joseph Papineau donated the square of land which still faces the present church of Saint-Jacques. Lartigue laid the cornerstone on May 22, 1823, in the presence of a handful of priests, none of them from Montreal.* His building was a two-story basilica, planned to be the largest church in Canada, with a seating capacity of three thousand. During construction an attempt was made to endow Saint-Jacques with the functions of a parish church so that it could hold baptisms, marriages, and funerals in addition to Mass. Characteristically, the wardens of Notre-Dame appealed not to Bishop Plessis but to Governor Sir Francis Burton in their successful attempt to retain their monopoly of such functions.[36]

But the building of the rival church could not be stayed. Bishop Plessis noted this with satisfaction just before his death in 1825: "God, who knows how to turn everything to his glory, Our very dear brothers, has taken advantage of the opposition by which Mgr. the Bishop of Telmesse has been tested since the beginning of his episcopate, to create in your city one more church, whose magnificent structure has raised itself as if by magic and which has come to completion with a speed which astonishes both visitors and local inhabitants."[37]

*The prevailing bitterness between the partisans of Lartigue and the Sulpicians was nicely summed up by the Curé of Notre-Dame when he said: "Certainly Monseigneur [Lartigue] will not be in need of stone, since everyone throws it at him." "Sans doute que Monseigneur ne doit pas être en peine de la pierre, car tout le monde la lui jette." (Romuald Trudeau, "Mes Tablettes," April 19, 1822.)

WITH THE REALIZATION that the incipient cathedral of Saint-Jacques would end their exclusive tenure of religious authority in Montreal, the Sulpicians and the wardens of Notre-Dame sought to regain lost ground. Since the followers of Auxiliary Bishop Lartigue exploited the fact that the only parish church in town was old, cramped, and poorly located, it seemed to the wardens that they had three possible courses of action: old Notre-Dame could be destroyed and a new church built; the old church could be retained but new branch churches built; or the old parish boundaries could be redrawn and many new parishes created.[1] Since the creation of branch congregations, either autonomous or quasi-autonomous, would inevitably weaken the centralized authority of the Sulpicians, the second and third alternatives were inadmissible. That left the first proposal: to keep Montreal as a single parish and build a giant new church to replace the old one on Place d'Armes. In fact, the city remained a single Sulpician parish until 1866, when it contained eighty thousand parishioners.[2] But the wardens hardly expected such a vigorous growth of Montreal. They estimated the Catholic population in 1822 at fifteen thousand and, based on past rates of growth, they expected that by 1872 the population might rise to thirty-three thousand. The report continued:

> but such a rise in the Catholic population of the parish is not at all probable. Your Committee believes that except for the important holidays, hardly a quarter of the parishioners should or could attend the parish High Mass at once, from which it is concluded that a church which could contain eight to nine thousand persons will in large measure suit the needs of the parish for *at least* fifty or sixty years to come.
>
> It has been calculated that a church which would be one hundred and twenty feet wide in the interior and two hundred feet long in the nave, not counting the choir, and having two tiers of galleries, could seat that number of people and at the same time enable everyone to hear the voice of the preacher.[3]

15

The wardens, without the aid of an architect, thus determined the basic shape and size of the new church. These specifications followed naturally from the available lands and funds, and the desired capacity. The site was also dictated by common sense. The new Sulpician church had to be located as closely as possible to the Seminary, even though it was no longer in the physical centre of Montreal. Place d'Armes had to be cleared for traffic, so that the next closest site was the south-east corner of Notre-Dame and Saint-Joseph Streets. On the land were a cemetery and four houses which could be purchased for £10,000 sterling. Additional land would be taken without cost from the gardens of the Seminary. The most curious feature of the report was the stipulation of double galleries. Double galleries were found at the back of many Quebec churches, but never on the sides. How these galleries might affect acoustics was presumably not considered by the wardens. Their main concern was financial.

The wardens had approximately £10,000 on hand to pay for the land. They expected that the church would cost £40,000. Twenty thousand pounds would be lent interest-free by the Seminary, and the remainder would be borrowed at 6 per cent, or on interest of £1,200 a year. It was anticipated that if the church revenue were £3,600 a year, the interest and 10 per cent of the principal could be repaid annually, and the church could liquidate its interest-bearing debt in ten years.[4] To raise this amount the committee decided that the church should rent twelve hundred pews. The arrangement at old Notre-Dame was to rent out the ground floor pews, but to allow free seats in the side gallery. In the new church both ground floor and side gallery pews would be rented out, but a second, free gallery would be added. Thus the most unusual feature of Notre-Dame, the second gallery, was determined not by architectural taste nor, strictly speaking, by capacity, but by a financial and social distinction in the pew system.

An unusual feature of the whole proceeding was the complete responsibility of laymen for the building of a Catholic church. The priests of the Seminary acted as both liturgical and artistic advisers, but apart from the gift of land and the loan of £10,000, they played no significant role in the construction of the new Notre-Dame. The wardens of Notre-Dame appointed certain members to a special building committee which took full charge of construction.

The fifteen members of this building committee were thus the real patrons of Notre-Dame. The nominal president was the Sulpician Candide-Michel LeSaulnier, curé of Notre-Dame from 1793 to 1830. Being sixty-five years old and in poor health, the curé infrequently attended committee meetings. French-born and a doctor of theology from the Sorbonne, LeSaulnier probably had some influence on the committee in matters of architectural taste, especially since he periodically revisited England and France.

The secretary was the retired fur trader François-Antoine LaRocque. As a young man LaRocque had explored the head-waters of the Missouri and the Rocky Mountains in order to open these territories to the Canadian fur trade. He was mentioned with respect several times in the journals of Lewis and Clark. He himself wrote two journals on his travels, and both were published. They show their author to be a man of keen intelligence and aggressiveness.[5] About 1818 he retired with a modest capital and settled in Montreal. He was elected chief warden of Notre-Dame, a director of the North West Company, a director of the Bank of Montreal, a harbour commissioner, and vice-president of the Montreal Savings Bank. He became a founder of the Montreal Fire Insurance Company, a director of the British and Canadian School, and a life governor of the Montreal General Hospital.[6] LaRocque and the multi-millionaire Joseph Masson were the only two men to sit on both of the most prestigious boards in Montreal: the vestry of Notre-Dame and the board of directors of the Bank of Montreal. His wife was the daughter of the prosperous fur trader Gabriel Côté, and his son married the granddaughter of the even wealthier Colonel Louis Guy. LaRocque presents the picture of a man thriving in an early retirement, keeping busy with such diversions as a business and pleasure trip to Europe in 1826 and the leadership of the building committee of Notre-Dame.

The building committee had two treasurers, Pierre de Rocheblave and François Desrivières. Pierre de Rastel, Sieur de Rocheblave, was a senior partner in the North West Company, a member of the Legislative Assembly and later of the Legislative Council of Quebec. His patrician family owned great tracts of land on the island of Montreal and in New Orleans. François Desrivières was the nephew and heir of the powerful fur trader James McGill and a man of considerable wealth until deprived of much of his land by McGill University.

The oldest and richest of the committeemen was Louis Guy, colonel-in-chief of the Militia on the island of Montreal and the most influential of the thirty-two magistrates who then administered the city. He had retained a seat on the vestry since 1796. Jean Bouthillier was another director of the Montreal Savings Bank. Jean-Phillipe Leprohon was a prominent magistrate in the civic administration. Nicholas-Benjamin Doucet was considered the most successful notary in Montreal and had written a widely read treatise on Canadian law. Alexis Laframboise was both a colonel in the Militia and a prosperous linen draper in Montreal.

Six men described as "notables de la Paroisse" were included on the committee because of their experience in commerce or in the building trade in

Montreal. Jules Quesnel was the only warden among them. He was a prominent lawyer, a future city councillor, a colonel in the Militia, and a director of the Montreal Savings Bank. Charles-Simon Delorme was an extensive landowner and director of the Banque du Peuple. Joseph Courcelles *dit* Chevalier was a mason-entrepreneur and builder of the old Montreal jail. Of the fifteen members of the building committee, the only men who would not qualify as the élite of Montreal were Chevalier and the three remaining builders, Pierre Pomminville, Pascal Comte, and Pascal Persillier *dit* Lachapelle.

The building committee had access to advice and aid on an informal basis from other prominent wardens: the banker Joseph Masson, the wealthy grain merchant Felixe Souligny, and the landowners Toussaint Pothier, John Delisle, and Olivier Berthelet. This group was in effect an oligarchy bound by marriage as well as common interest. LaRocque, Quesnel, and Laframboise were brothers-in-law, and marriage related Laframboise and de Rocheblave, LaRocque and Guy, Guy and Berthelet.

It is significant that these committeemen represented not the traditional professions but the merchant class of French Canada, a class whose very existence was denied until recently. These men had the audacity to challenge the English commercial supremacy; the lines of commerce attracted them to London, New York, and Boston much more than the lines of sentiment to Paris.[7] They mixed with and competed with the English, but they had no wish to be assimilated by them. When the English proposed the Bill of Union in 1822, a giant rally on the Champs de Mars elected an *ad hoc* committee to fight for French-Canadian rights. Of the seventeen men on the committee, five were on the building committee of Notre-Dame: Louis Guy, the president, as well as Jules Quesnel, Jean Bouthillier, François-Antoine LaRocque, and François Desrivières.[8] Their aggressiveness, their self-made but slightly *arriviste* quality, and above all, the equivocal position of these men as *Québécois* in an English-speaking world were to have most important consequences for the style of their new church.

At first the committee met with opposition from Quebec City. LaRocque asked Bishop Plessis several times for permission to build a new church, but Plessis insisted that the petition come from the priests and not from the lay wardens.[9] In the end, however, Plessis proved remarkably docile. He had been known, as in the case of the parish of Saint-Pierre-les-Becquets, to insist on the site of a new church even over the trenchant opposition of the curé and wardens.[10] In this case, he had the right to choose the site and to approve or reject the plans of the new church of Notre-Dame, but he agreed to its construction without being consulted on either the site or the plans of the building.

In the intervening year between the preliminary decision to build in September 1822 and the appointment of the permanent building committee in September 1823, there seems to have been a change in the concept of the new Notre-Dame. The report of September 1822 was rather austere in its concept of what was needed. It referred to cost, seating capacity, and pew revenues and laid out plans for an unpromising rectangular box with double galleries. There was no discussion of aesthetics except in the matter of acoustics. But conditions were possibly better than the wardens realized. They acquired the four Saint-Joseph Street properties for slightly less than the £10,000 they had estimated, and the first fund-raising campaign of August 1823 brought in another £10,000. This was a sizeable sum, considering that many Montrealers resented what they called the secrecy and cliquishness of the wardens.[11] The state of Montreal was also one of well-being. The prosperity that began with the war of 1812 would continue only until the depression of 1826 and the collapse of the Montreal-based North West Company. But no one could foresee this in the prosperous years of 1822-23. Prosperity, coupled with the threat to French-Canadian survival posed by the Bill of Union of 1822, encouraged the wardens to think of the church in terms of exceptional magnificence as a monument to their race. In June 1823 Curé LeSaulnier disclosed that the seating capacity of the church would be not eight but ten thousand. He exhorted his parishioners to build the most beautiful church in all America, which would be, he said, an eternal reminder to their descendants of the good taste, the generosity, and the piety of its builders.[12]

The desire to make Notre-Dame a monumental church was stressed in the resolution of the wardens concerning the choice of an architect. It appears that local architects were *a priori* disqualified — an ironic decision for the building destined to be the national monument of French Canada. The wardens instructed the building committee "to bring over an architect from the United States or from Europe, if it seems suitable."[13] Within a week a letter was sent to M. Thavenet, a Sulpician in Paris, requesting the names of the best available French architects.[14]

The fact that local architects were not considered for Notre-Dame is consistent with the character of the wardens as self-made men engaged in a struggle with the English merchant class. Not learned in architecture, they nevertheless wanted their church to rival the best of those in Europe and America. The church of Mgr. Lartigue was large, but it was a plain and old-fashioned building, the creation of a local master mason. Its interior was a two-story basilica on the lines of Saint-Denis-sur-Richelieu, the late eighteenth-century rural church in which Lartigue had been ordained in 1800. The exterior of Lartigue's church of Saint-Jacques was a crude attempt to reproduce the twin towers and the portico of Saint-Sulpice in Paris.[15] Because it was such an undistinguished building, the cathedral excited no special admiration in the city of Montreal. Notre-Dame had to do better than that.

If Notre-Dame was to be an outstanding building, its architect had to be chosen with care. The first impulse had been to import an architect from Paris, but long before they received a reply from Thavenet, the building committee sent Jean Bouthillier, one of their semi-retired members, to hire the best available architect in New York. As soon as he arrived in New York early in September 1823, Bouthillier sought the advice of two of his business contacts, the merchants John Proctor and Lewis Willcocks. Willcocks was a leading Catholic layman in New York, and served as legal representative for Notre-Dame in that city. He had received his education at the Sulpicians' own Collège de Montréal and kept in close touch with his old friends in Canada.[16] Both Proctor and Willcocks recommended James O'Donnell, a friend of theirs, for the architect of Notre-Dame.[17] Proctor apparently arranged a meeting with Bouthillier; Willcocks probably added his recommendations later.

O'Donnell's qualifications, however, spoke for themselves. He was the designer of at least four major buildings in New York besides a number of houses. His last building was a Gothic church which had opened just three months earlier to much acclaim. Although O'Donnell had never designed a Catholic church, Bouthillier was sufficiently impressed with his works and unexecuted projects to invite him to come for an interview in Montreal. On his return Bouthillier gave an account of his mission to the building committee:

> Mr. Bouthillier reported that upon his arrival in New York, he made the acquaintance of an architect who was said to be very able, and who had been strongly recommended to him as a person very capable of furnishing the necessary plans for the construction of our new Church, and that this architect was known here by Mr. Vanderlyn, from whom one could have additional information on the subject.
> Messrs. LaRocque and Quesnel are instructed accordingly to see Mr. Vanderlyn and to receive from him information on the capacity and talents of Mr. O'Donnell, the architect in question.[18]

It was the good fortune of O'Donnell that John Vanderlyn, a celebrated painter and one of his closest friends in New York, had chosen that same month to hold an exhibition in Montreal.[19] On September 19, 1823, Vanderlyn sent this enthusiastic endorsement to secretary LaRocque:

D. SIR,

As I calculate on leaving this for New-York on Sunday Morning — I shall be happy to take any communication you may wish further to make Mr. O'Donnell on the subject of your plans for a New Church.

As I am on terms of friendship and intimacy with Mr. O'Donnell I confess I should be gratified to see him employed in the project. In which case, I shall take an interest and pleasure in furnishing him with what ideas I possess on the subject.

I question whether you can find a better man than Mr. O'Donnell on this side the Atlantic for your purpose.

I am very respectfully,
Your most Obedᵗ. Serᵗ.

Friday, 19th Sepᵗ.

Jɴ. Vᴀɴᴅᴇʀʟʏɴ

𝕿HE BUILDING COMMITTEE insisted that two basic requirements be met in the construction of Notre-Dame. The church must be big enough to seat eight to nine thousand people, and it must look magnificent. And although James O'Donnell had been selected somewhat by chance, he seemed to be the architect whose training and style of design could satisfy these requirements.

The career of O'Donnell spanned the Atlantic. He was born in 1774 as the only son of a fairly prosperous, land-owning family in County Wexford, Ireland. His family, who had emigrated from County Donegal in the north, had attained a certain social standing and bore a coat of arms. Before the birth of O'Donnell, they had been converted from the Catholic to the Anglican church.[1] After a minimum of formal education, O'Donnell seems to have made his way to Dublin and there apprenticed himself to an established architect.

Eighteenth-century Dublin was an ideal European city for architectural training. The English aristocracy who filled the viceregal court commissioned hundreds of buildings for public and private functions. The Bank of Ireland, the Four Courts, the Customs House, and the row houses on Merrion and Kildare Squares stand today as splendid examples of the late Georgian style.[2] Beginning with Lord Burlington, who personally encouraged the neo-Palladian style in Ireland, a succession of capable and sometimes brilliant architects came from England and the continent to serve the discriminating aristocracy of Dublin. Chief among them were Sir William Chambers, his pupils James Gandon and Thomas Cooley, and Cooley's pupil Francis Johnston, who carried on the Georgian style until his death in 1829.[3]

There is only one known drawing made by James O'Donnell in the years of his apprenticeship. It is a plan and elevation for a mausoleum, designed at

James O'Donnell

the age of twenty-four.[4] The mausoleum was to have had a subterranean tomb chamber, a two-story square base, an octagon, and a saucer dome (*Plate 5*). The design is conceived as a massive form with only token superficial ornament: a niche, garlands, four pinnacles, and an iron balustrade about the oculus of the dome.

Nothing definite is known about O'Donnell from the age of twenty-four to thirty-eight. This period in his development can be plausibly recreated by analogy with the career of a man just fifteen years his senior, Francis Johnston. Johnston, like O'Donnell, had left his middle-class rural family to take his apprenticeship in Dublin. By 1790 he had become the first Irish-born and Irish-trained architect of distinction.[5] Johnston worked in three main styles: neo-classical in the manner of Sir William Chambers for churches and great public buildings; Adamesque and Regency for houses and less formal commissions, and Gothic Revival for some churches and other special projects.[6] O'Donnell's own buildings would later fall into roughly the same three categories.

Johnston's involvement in the Gothic Revival is especially significant. In 1796 he visited England for three weeks and closely examined its medieval Gothic cathedrals and its Gothic Revival churches. When he returned to Ireland, he became the first practitioner of Gothic Revival in that country.[7] His finest work in Gothic was the Chapel Royal in Dublin Castle (1807-1814) (*Plate 22*). Its well-preserved interior is a plaster and wood confection of ribbed vaults over the nave, fan vaults over the side aisles, an ornate gallery fringed with drop tracery, stucco ornament, and a pointed east window subdivided by lacy wooden mullions. The Chapel constitutes one of the loveliest examples of Rococo Gothic in the British Isles.

Did O'Donnell study under Francis Johnston? The impression that he did is almost inescapable, though not yet documented. Two churches which played a large role in O'Donnell's design for Notre-Dame were Johnston's Chapel Royal and James Gibbs's St. Martin's-in-the-Fields, London.* As a resident of Dublin until 1812, possibly as an assistant to Johnston, O'Donnell had five years in which to study the Chapel Royal, and ten years in which to examine Johnston's St. George's Church, a close copy of St. Martin's.[8] When he began work on Notre-Dame, O'Donnell showed exceptional ability in estimating materials and labour needed for construction, in drafting detailed drawings for the workmen, and in organizing hundreds of subordinates. One would assume that this kind of ability came from previous experience as a builder, but in the United States O'Donnell practised only as a designer of plans and not as a builder. It is therefore likely that his building experience was gained in Ireland, probably under Johnston. In 1805 Johnston was appointed Archi-

*See Chapter V, pp. 35 and 36.

24

tect to the Board of Works and virtually dominated public architecture in Ireland.[9] If we assume that O'Donnell served as one of Johnston's numerous assistants, many peculiarities of his later style may be explained. Foremost is the discrepancy between the richness and vitality of his detailed drawings and the routine quality of his overall architectonic conceptions. As an assistant O'Donnell would have worked closely with builders and with decorators, but he would have had less experience in total composition.[10] This imbalance in his training later emerged at Notre-Dame.

In a letter to the building committee, March 16, 1824, O'Donnell claimed: "I have studied under some of the first Masters, and have carefully examined some of the best monuments in Europe, France excepted which I have not been in." All the available evidence suggests that both these claims are exaggerated. O'Donnell might have worked for James Gandon, the most distinguished architect in Ireland, until the latter's retirement in 1808, but there is little stylistic affinity to suggest that he did. So O'Donnell's reference to the "first Masters" probably alludes to Francis Johnston and his brother Richard, both capable and active men but not brilliant designers. There are no exhibition records and no references in O'Donnell's correspondence to suggest that he lived for any extended period in England. Although there is no reason to doubt O'Donnell's statement that he had travelled through Europe, neither his letters nor his works give evidence that such a tour was crucial to his architectural development.

O'Donnell turned thirty-eight in 1812 and still had no great building to his credit. For twenty-five years England had been at war or preparing for war with France. The building trades stagnated with the shift of public funds to military activity; a financial depression curtailed private building to the same degree. O'Donnell therefore emigrated to New York, where for fourteen years he carried on a successful practice. There are ten buildings which can be securely attributed to him: the renovation and extension of Columbia College (1817-20); Bloomingdale Asylum (1818-21); the Fulton Street Market (1821-22); Christ Church on Anthony Street (1822-23); the First Presbyterian Church in Rochester (1823-24); his own house which still stands at 2 Oliver Street, New York (1821); and four elegant town houses on State Street opposite the Battery (1816) (*Plates 6, 7, 8*).[11]

Of the five main buildings planned by O'Donnell before Notre-Dame, the two churches are less interesting and less capably designed than the public buildings. The college, the asylum, and the market follow the conventional pattern of late Georgian facades in alternating planes of recession and projection, with simple window frames and a relatively uncluttered roofline. The massive portico in the proposed elevation for Columbia College suggests that

James O'Donnell

O'Donnell was not too successful in depicting elegance, but his classical designs show at least a high degree of competence.

O'Donnell was less successful in his designs for Gothic churches. In this he was typical of the period. His contemporary Joseph Mangin could turn from the neo-classical elegance of his New York City Hall to the naïve Gothic of St. Patrick's Old Cathedral in the same city. John McComb, co-designer of the City Hall, did as badly in ten plans and elevations which he made in 1823 for a church in the Gothic style.[12] The Gothic designs of Benjamin Henry Latrobe, America's foremost architect, appear to us today as much inferior to his works in the Classical Revival.

O'Donnell was experimenting in Gothic style in the year that he met Bouthillier. He had just completed Christ Church in New York and was improving the design for a second commission in Rochester. Christ Church was a Georgian Gothic building of heavy proportions. The facade appeared to be almost crushed beneath the weight of the high entablature and pediment. The front was subdivided into three rectangles by squat pilasters, and a window and a door were placed almost aimlessly within each unit. Only in the centre bay, in which the window was made contiguous with the architrave of the door, was there an attempt to adapt the smaller elements in the design to the main lines of the facade. Over the front was a severe two-story tower which cut rather gracelessly through the pediment.

The First Presbyterian Church of Rochester (1823-24) was a distinct improvement over Christ Church and slightly better in quality than the average American church of this early stage in the Gothic Revival. It was 86 feet long, 64 feet wide and 30 feet high. Although this church, like Christ Church, was conceived as a meeting house with Gothic detail, an attempt was made to break from the classical ideal of an equilibrium of forces and to emphasize the verticality of the facade. The tower, for example, projected 3 feet from the plane of the facade and rose 150 feet from the base of the church. The roof seems to have been hipped rather than pitched, so that there was no gable to be incorporated into the facade. O'Donnell thus avoided the pedimented Greek temple-front appearance which had caused such awkwardness in the design of Christ Church in New York. It is probable, but not certain, that he also designed the embattled parapet over the facade. The high, thin pilasters, the spire, and the amalgamation of windows and doors into three tall units contributed to a sense of verticality in the facade. O'Donnell had also improved upon the design of his earlier church by reducing the height of the entablatures, by integrating details with the mass, and by simplifying the composition. There was, however, a curious regression in the use of two rows of short windows on the flanks of the First Presbyterian Church, rather than a single row of high pointed openings as in Christ Church.

The interiors of the two churches differed to some degree. The interior of the First Presbyterian Church was arranged as an amphitheatre, the centre of which was the pulpit. Not only was the floor sloped like a theatre, but also the gallery, supported by Ionic columns, was set at an incline. Nothing indicates the presence of Gothic ornament inside the First Presbyterian, perhaps because O'Donnell prepared only the exterior design. Christ Church, on the other hand, was specifically and ostentatiously Gothic. Again the floor and galleries were inclined, but the columns and ornament were in the Gothic manner. A contemporary guide stated: "The pulpit, canopy, and altar are in a style bordering on the florid Gothic, and of most exquisite workmanship. The architect was James O'Donnell."[13] O'Donnell was not the builder of Christ Church, but he did supply drawings throughout its construction.[14] The small but frequent payments he received and the specific mention in the guide book suggest that O'Donnell designed all the furnishings of Christ Church. If so, his imagination clearly expressed itself there, as at Notre-Dame, in much richer conceptions of detail than of overall design.

O'Donnell built large and expensive buildings in the classical style. The Fulton Street Market cost $150,000, the Bloomingdale Asylum over $200,000. But he dreamed of even larger buildings in Gothic style. For the time being these projects took shape only in drawings which he exhibited in 1816, 1817, and 1818 at the American Academy of the Fine Arts in New York. Out of a total of twenty-eight designs, fifteen were drawings for a "Gothic Cathedral" seen from every angle.[15] One of the drawings shown in 1816 was a "Design for the front of a College, in the Gothic style." Other drawings related to his Bloomingdale Asylum commission, some to the houses on State Street, and the remainder to unspecified public and private buildings. An American architect who devoted so much time to a cathedral and college in the Gothic style as early as 1816 must be considered a pioneer Gothic Revival enthusiast. The design for a Gothic college immediately suggests that O'Donnell influenced or was influenced by Professor James Renwick, Sr. Renwick had prepared three designs in 1813 for the rebuilding of Columbia College in the style of King's College Chapel at Cambridge.[16] O'Donnell and Renwick worked together on the renovation of Columbia College in 1817, the former as architect and the latter as the leading member of the building committee. Probably to the displeasure of both, the old eighteenth-century building was refurbished but not replaced, so that a Gothic design was out of the question.

From what is now known of his career, it appears that O'Donnell was a capable architect with experience in designing very large projects. Equally important, his personal preference in style seems to have been Gothic. O'Donnell worked in the usual sort of "Meeting House Gothic" found at that time

James O'Donnell   in the United States but, at least in interior details, he could recall and recreate the more lavish "Rococo Gothic" he had known in Ireland. In a sense then, O'Donnell's career was a suitable preliminary for the design of Notre-Dame, in which great size could be coupled with the Gothic style to create the building which had existed in his mind for nearly a decade.

O'DONNELL gave some thought to the design of Notre-Dame even before coming to Montreal.[1] He arrived from New York on October 3, 1823, and just six days later described his preliminary plans to the wardens.* After ten days spent in surveying the site of the church, examining stone in the quarries, and discussing the project with LaRocque and Quesnel, O'Donnell drew up detailed sketches of the interior and exterior (*Plate* 9).[2] The sketches were submitted to the building committee on October 14, and its minutes show they were formally accepted three days later. After seventy-three years of discussion of a new church, the plans of Notre-Dame were thus approved with remarkable speed.

O'Donnell was faced with the problem of planning a church two to three times larger than any other that stood in America. The building committee gave him the general dimensions it wanted and told him where to build the church, how much to spend, and how quickly to proceed. But there was no recorded discussion between architect and patrons on matters of style. Left a relatively free agent, O'Donnell was able to incorporate into his design for Notre-Dame features of other buildings which he had admired. O'Donnell's final design was an original creation but, had he not utilized many sources of inspiration, his Montreal church would have been only a variant of his modest churches in New York and Rochester. And that is what almost happened.

Between the first and second meetings of the building committee, O'Donnell's plans were publicly exhibited in the window of notary N.-B. Doucet's

---

*The wardens had requested that the nave be 120 feet wide and 200 feet long, excluding the choir. O'Donnell's first plan for the nave was reported to be 128 feet wide and 200 feet long, with a choir 75 feet deep. (Louis-Adolphe Huguet-Latour, *Annuaire de Ville-Marie*, p. 398, quoting from the minutes of the wardens' committee, October 9, 1823.)

office on Notre-Dame Street. They occasioned a lengthy description in a local
English paper:

> We have been favoured with a cursory inspection of plan and elevation of
> the new Catholic Church proposed to be built in this city; and we feel highly
> gratified in being able to report that, as a whole, the plan is of a character which
> well entitles it to the approbation of the public, no less as an architectural dis-
> play of external taste and ornament, than in internal usefulness and convenience.
> The front, which is to run parallel with Notre-Dame Street, will be 150 feet in
> length, and will be composed of plain cut stone in the simple gothic style, ter-
> minating in two splendid square towers, 194 feet in extreme height and 90 feet
> asunder. Each front of these towers is decorated with the dial plate of a clock.
> There are three grand entrances in front, finely ornamented in the true gothic
> style, supported by square massy pillasters [sic] of the same order. These en-
> trances are surmounted by three corresponding windows, over which the main
> front terminates in a fine row of embrasures 90 feet long, at the extremities of
> which the towers begin to be distinguished. The length of the building from
> front to rear, we believe, is 253 feet, and is finished in a manner worthy of so
> fine a front. Each of these longitudinal walls contains a gothic door, and is sur-
> mounted at the extreme termination with a neat gothic tower. The interior
> seems to be commodiously and appropriately laid out, and is made to contain,
> between the floor and the gallery, thirteen hundred pews. Spacious accommoda-
> tion is reserved for the great altar; and every exertion is made to combine taste-
> ful arrangement with utility. It is proposed to warm the Church in winter by
> means of heated air, which we deem a better and a safer method than by stoves.
> From the slight inspection which we have had of this interesting plan, it is im-
> possible to convey a more perfect idea of its beauty & dimensions but we think
> it highly deserving of public encouragement, as conferring on this city a lasting
> public ornament of architectural elegance (*Montreal Gazette*, October 18,
> 1823).

These plans are now lost. O'Donnell, in a letter to the building committee
on March 16, 1824, disparagingly called them "a few rough sketches," but in
fact they were not at all rough, and they had an important bearing on the final
design of the church. Most importantly, the plans show that the church was
to be the first major building in the Gothic style in Canada. The wardens' im-
mediate approval of O'Donnell's Gothic design was thus a landmark decision
in the architectural history of Quebec and perhaps of all Canada.* But the plan
itself was quite commonplace for O'Donnell. He proposed to make Notre-
Dame an amalgam of various features from his Christ Church in New York
and the First Presbyterian Church in Rochester (*Plate* 9). Three windows
over three doors and thick pilasters as at Christ Church and an embattled parapet and square towers with a clock face as at First Presbyterian were proposed. There were just two features in the elevation which O'Donnell had not

*See Chapter IX.

used before: an arcaded terrace on the side (described only in the minutes of the building committee) and twin towers on the facade.

The idea of placing twin towers at the ends of a flat or embattled parapet was not new. It had appeared in France about 1800, William Strickland had used it in his St. Stephen's Church in Philadelphia in 1822-23, and there was a much earlier precedent in the facade of Notre-Dame in Paris.[3] Although O'Donnell's facade was to have been big (150 feet wide and perhaps 110 feet high), there was little to make it look magnificent. The bareness of the facade suggests that O'Donnell at first thought of enlarging the size of his earlier churches without facing up to the problems and the opportunities offered by composing on such a large scale.

In mid-October O'Donnell returned to his home in New York, where for six months he worked on a second, more detailed set of plans for Notre-Dame. During these six months many letters were exchanged between the architect and the patrons in Montreal, but very little was said about the evolution of O'Donnell's plans. The correspondence centred mainly on the salary and duties of the architect. O'Donnell signed a contract with the committee on May 4, 1824, in which he agreed to take up permanent residence in Montreal in order to direct construction and to supply all the necessary working drawings.* The architect was to receive $1,500 (£375) a year for four years, of which $500 would be held in reserve annually by the committee to guarantee fulfilment of the contract.

In April 1824 O'Donnell informed the editor of *The Albion,* a New York newspaper, that he had completed plans for Notre-Dame. In an article of April 3, 1824, the paper reported that "a magnificent edifice is about to be erected at Montreal, surpassing in magnitude and splendour any upon the continent of North America." The report called the style of the church "strictly and purely gothic, from the best models now existing in Europe" and estimated construction costs at four hundred thousand dollars. In May, O'Donnell presented his detailed plans to the committee in Montreal, and the minutes of May 14, 1824, show they were approved with the addition of two specific alterations made by the architect: the placing of salient buttresses on the flanks and the insertion of staircases at the east end of the nave. The records of the committee refer to no other changes in the design.

Apart from models in wood which were occasionally made for the instruction of the workmen, O'Donnell set down his proposals for Notre-Dame in drawings.[4] One hundred and seventy-three designs from the hand of O'Donnell still exist in Notre-Dame. Four of these are wash drawings the architect made to convey his ideas to the wardens. The rest are pen-and-ink designs of details, sometimes in full scale, which were shown to the workmen. The

*See Appendix B for the full text of O'Donnell's contract.

sheets were frequently fastened with sealing wax to a carpenter's bench and pricked for transfer. O'Donnell later complained that workmen had stolen many of these drawings; hundreds or thousands of them must have been destroyed during construction.[5]

From drawings, letters, and contemporary comments, it is possible to reconstruct the evolution of the design of Notre-Dame. O'Donnell presumably began by devising a ground plan to suit the land available. The rectangle at the south-east corner of Saint-Joseph and Notre-Dame Streets had been purchased and was about to be cleared. It was 165 feet wide on Place d'Armes and extended east about 300 feet down the slope of Saint-Joseph Street. The site was far from ideal. The first difficulty was that it was off-centre with respect to Place d'Armes (*Plate* 10). O'Donnell hoped to regularize the trapezoid of Place d'Armes into a square and to place the church closer to the Seminary on the south.[6] This was within his power since the *Fabrique*, or corporation of Notre-Dame, owned the square. But the wardens were not inclined to waste land in order to improve the appearance of the church, and O'Donnell's suggestion was ignored.

In his definitive plan of the crypt, O'Donnell indicated two spacious terraces which were to flank the church (*Plate* 11). The first was provided simply by chance. The old church of Notre-Dame had a transept and several sacristies which spread east of Notre-Dame Street. If the new church were placed close to Notre-Dame Street, a large part of the old church would have been destroyed, and the congregation would have needed temporary quarters for worship. The new church was therefore set back forty feet from the street and incidentally acquired one of its most pleasant characteristics. O'Donnell also wanted to erect another terrace on Saint-Joseph Street which would accentuate rather than ignore the fifteen-foot drop in ground level from the front to the back of the church. The committee had already rejected the first proposal for an arcade beneath the terrace; now in 1824 or 1825 O'Donnell suggested that the terrace rest on a series of nine compartments. The wedge-shaped terrace would have disguised the obtuse angle of Notre-Dame and Saint-Joseph Streets and provided a promenade above the storehouses or burial vaults below (*Plate* 25). Unfortunately money ran out before this terrace could be built.

The plan of the crypt also represents a basement corridor along the south flank of the church. Following the arrangement at old Notre-Dame, this corridor would have led from the Seminary to the back of the church so that the priests could file quietly into the choir stalls from behind the altar and so avoid an ostentatious procession down the main aisle. A two-story sacristy was proposed for the south-east corner (*Plate* 32). Neither the corridor nor the sacristy was built because of lack of funds. Only in 1850 was a corridor constructed from the Seminary to the centre bay of the south wall, and in 1892 a sacristy was erected at almost the exact spot that O'Donnell had indicated seventy years earlier.

The crypt of the church was a simple rectangle measuring 255 feet in length and 136 feet in width. In each corner of the rectangle O'Donnell indicated square partitions to carry staircases up to the galleries. The squares at the west end were made especially thick to carry the front towers. Between the towers was a recessed portico 69 feet wide and 20 feet deep. Two square bases were provided for the octagonal piers on the open side of the portico. The walls were made of rough-dressed stone 5 feet thick and strengthened with buttresses at intervals of approximately 27 feet. The basement was left as a single unpartitioned space in order to provide 1,200 burial plots. This was important to the wardens as a continuation of an ancient tradition and as a source of very considerable revenue. The practice of burial in the crypt of Notre-Dame was discontinued only at mid-century by order of the courts. Three large burial vaults directly beneath the sanctuary were assigned to the clergy. Forty-two stone piers, 3 feet in diameter and 9 feet high, were provided for the support of half-trunks of oak which carried the ground floor. Sixteen larger piers acted as supports for the wooden columns of the nave. Two more were provided for columns beneath the organ loft at the west end.

The ground floor of Notre-Dame took its general shape from a common form of English and American churches of the eighteenth and nineteenth centuries (*Plate* 12). This was a rectangle almost twice as long as wide, with a shallow oblong vestibule leading into a broad nave with side galleries. Flanking the vestibule were corner squares containing staircases to the gallery. At the east end there was a similar square-and-oblong arrangement with the oblong used as a chancel and the squares as vestry and robing rooms. The plan originated in Georgian churches, but was adapted to the Gothic style as well.[7] It was the basis for many and perhaps most of the six hundred Greek and Gothic Revival churches erected in England under the Church Building Act of 1818.[8] The popularity of the plan was exported to America in the early nineteenth century by means of Gothic Revival handbooks.[9]

Although the plan of Notre-Dame was thus fairly common, evidence points to the existence of a specific precedent. In April 1824 François-Antoine LaRocque conferred in Montreal with John Proctor, O'Donnell's friend from New York. LaRocque then reported to the building committee: "This gentleman says that the plans of our church are generally approved and that a church is already being built on the same plan in New York, but smaller in dimensions."[10]

The minutes do not specify which New York church, but this information may be inferred. The most distinguished church to be built in New York in the years 1823-25 was St. Thomas Church on Broadway. It became famous as the first successful application of Gothic structural methods in America.[11] Its architect was the Irishman Josiah Brady (*c.* 1760-1832), who had worked in New York at the same time and in the same range of styles as O'Donnell. St. Thomas Church was approximately sixty feet wide and one hundred feet long. It had a shallow oblong vestibule flanked by square lobbies at the west end and a convex sanctuary railing, a square vestry room, and a square "waiting room" at the east end.[12] Notre-Dame was proportionally somewhat longer than St. Thomas, but the resemblance between the two plans is striking. The four corner rooms of St. Thomas were used as stairtowers at Notre-Dame; the oblong vestibule was transformed into an open portico. But one telling feature, the curved sanctuary, was employed in a similar manner in both churches.

Like the site, the interior dimensions which the building committee had chosen and imposed on the architect were less than ideal. By a curious co-incidence, the preaching box which the vestry had stipulated in its report of 1822 most closely resembled a Huguenot temple. Salomon de Brosse's famous temple at Charenton was a similar rectangle twice as long as wide with canted double galleries on all four sides.[13] The building committee was only willing to pay for a utilitarian structure like a Huguenot auditorium, but they expected the architect to provide them with something magnificent.

The interior of Notre-Dame is 215 feet long and 121 feet, 8 inches wide. As an unpartitioned space, this interior might have been a low, broad hall of lifeless proportions. Faced with a similar problem, Josiah Brady had disguised the box-like aspect of the nave of St. Thomas by constructing an open hammer-beam roof, which became the architectural sensation of New York.[14] Rather than disguise the essential features of his nave, O'Donnell emphasized them as the cornerstone of an imaginative design. Through manipulation of the columns, the galleries, and the ceiling, he enhanced the depth and verticality of the nave.

The role of the columns and double galleries was especially important. The fourteen free-standing columns partition the interior into a nave, sixty-seven feet wide, and two side aisles each twenty-seven feet, four inches wide. Because of the pronounced curve of the ceiling and the prominence of the gallery fronts which are strung between the columns, visual emphasis is placed on the nave. The observer tends to overlook the total breadth of the interior and to concentrate on the proportionally narrower nave.

It appears that O'Donnell next exploited a technique of the painter to create a sense of greater depth in the nave. The emphasis on the gallery fronts encourages the observer to see the nave of Notre-Dame in terms of lines rather than mass. The interior then becomes a giant perspective grid, with the gallery fronts acting as orthogonals which converge at a vanishing point in the sanctuary. The pronounced slope of the floor contributes markedly to this perspective effect (*Plate* 21). But to continue the analogy with painting, the nave is conceived not according to Albertian perspective but in imitation of the "forced" perspective of the Mannerists. The columns are not spaced at uniform intervals as one expects, but there is a progressive diminution in the width of the bays from the middle to the east end of the nave. As O'Donnell's plan of the crypt shows, the middle bay before the pulpit is thirty feet wide, the three succeeding bays twenty-seven feet wide, the last bay to the east just twenty-two feet wide. Standing in the nave, the diminution of the bays seems to be an optical illusion caused by the great length of the interior. Since there was no structural necessity for the divergent width of the bays, and since O'Donnell manipulated the placing of the exterior buttresses for the same effect, one could assume that the unconventional handling of the columns was intended as an optical illusion to enhance the length of the nave.

For the illusion of greater height O'Donnell utilized the columns and the ceiling. Most American churches of his time had galleries, but these galleries were usually constructed like balconies which were held up by columns underneath. The balconies were structurally independent from the nave and looked like an afterthought to the main design. For the galleries of Notre-Dame O'Donnell reverted to a style which had appeared at least a century earlier, notably in James Gibbs's church of St. Martin's-in-the-Fields, London (1722-26). Gibbs had integrated the galleries into the structure of the church by devising columns which rose in a single order from the floor, through the gallery fronts, and up to the ceiling. O'Donnell perhaps followed Gibbs in the arrangement of the galleries and in resting the ceiling directly on the columns, without the usual intermediary of a continuous entablature (*Plates* 20, 21).* He could have studied the structural system of St. Martin's either through the cross-sections in Gibbs's enormously influential *A Book of Architecture* (London, 1728) or indirectly through two derivative churches, St. George's in Dublin and St. Paul's Chapel in New York. O'Donnell also tried to suggest the reciprocal relationship of load and support between the ceiling and the columns by extending the cluster of colonnettes into a cluster of ribs on the vault (*Plate* 18).

The unbroken line of the columns and the pseudo-vaults of the ceiling exaggerated the impression of verticality in the nave. The ceiling of Notre-Dame is a plaster and lathe construction which is suspended from the roof (*Plate* 36). It is a barrel vault rising from the capitals to its crown, eighty feet above the floor. The vault has a continuous surface except for the sixteen-foot-

*There are further similarities in the proportions of the nave, the profile of the ceiling, the prominence of the window in the altar wall, and the elaborate tracery of the vaults, although in Notre-Dame all these features are Gothicized.

high openings between the columns. There are no serveries between the ribs. O'Donnell proposed to simulate recessions by applying a network of fan tracery to the ceiling. Areas crowded with tracery would seem to project; areas relatively free of tracery would seem to recede (*Plate* 19). When lack of funds forced cancellation of the rib vaulting, O'Donnell directed a painter to colour the "projecting" vaults grey and the "recessed" vaults black. This colouration achieved a similar illusion of ribbed vaulting, according to photographs and sketches of the time. The O'Donnell ceiling plan was partially executed a generation later, and still provides a fairly convincing illusion of ribbed vaulting (*Plate* 21).

The ceiling plan was one of several early American attempts to duplicate English fan vaulting, such as one finds in the chapel of Henry VII in Westminster Abbey, with the substitution here of columns for the pendants in the original. John Milner's *Treatise on the Ecclesiastical Architecture of England* (London, 1811) contained a view of the chapel which was the model for a fan-vaulted ceiling in Pittsburgh in 1823.[15] O'Donnell's ceiling, had it been executed, would have had greater lightness and intricacy than any then existing in America. The use of quadrapartite vaults over the nave and fan vaults over the side aisles indicates that a secondary source for this plan may have been the plasterwork ceiling of Johnston's Chapel Royal in Dublin (*Plate* 22).*

The fourth feature to which O'Donnell gave special care was the sanctuary. Although more radically transformed than any other part of the church since the death of O'Donnell, the east end of the nave retains in essence the lines of the 1825 arrangement which he prepared (*Plates* 12, 13). O'Donnell planned the sanctuary to be sixty-seven feet wide and fifty-one feet deep. The front was isolated from the nave by five steps and a railing in the form of what he called a *cyma reversa* (reverse curve); the back was a broad horseshoe of choir stalls. Here one assumes that the wardens simply instructed O'Donnell to reproduce the arrangement in old Notre-Dame.[16] The altar was at first intended to be free-standing, as it had been at old Notre-Dame until 1814, and as it still is today at Saint-Sulpice in Paris.† When O'Donnell later incorporated the altar into the line of the choir stalls, he also changed its shape to give it an unmistakable resemblance to the plan of the altar in Saint-Sulpice (*Plate* 40).[17]

---

*Other possible relationships between Notre-Dame and the Chapel Royal are found in the arrangement of a raised sanctuary flanked by blind arches and stairtowers, in the form of the capitals and shafts of the columns, and in the profusion of drop tracery on the soffits of the gallery fronts.

†Baron de la Hontan said of old Notre-Dame in 1684: "It is built on the model of the church of Saint-Sulpice in Paris and the altar is free-standing in the same way." "Elle est bâtie sur le modèle de celle de Saint-Sulpice de Paris, et l'autel est pareillement isolé." (Baron de la Hontan, *Voyages au Canada*, p. 46.)

The plan of 1825 seems to indicate an ambulatory behind the choir stalls. The side aisles were to be terminated by two side chapels backed up against the square wooden stairtowers. The function of the towers is curious in that the public would have entered directly from the outside to the stairs and up to the galleries without being able to enter the nave. The stairtowers on the ground floor were removed many years later, leaving a slight protrusion in the wall near the north-east door. When the idea of a separate sacristy was abandoned, the ambulatory had to be blocked off for the use of the priests. O'Donnell then made a second partition to flank the stairtowers and substituted a blind for an open arch in the last bay on the east. These alterations must have been made during construction, since the form of the original open arch is still visible in the attic above the ceiling.

The ill-fated climax of the sanctuary was the great window in the eastern wall. It measured thirty-two feet wide and sixty-four feet high. In its general effect the window was successful in that it focused attention on its tall, pointed shape and away from the broad, low profile of the nave. But either O'Donnell underestimated the amount of light it would admit, or the wardens would not buy stained glass to act as a filter, for its blinding light was so disturbing that the bottom fifteen feet were blocked off about 1850, and the rest of it was suppressed thirty-five years later.

Designing the exterior of Notre-Dame was a more complex process than arranging the interior because the outside had to relate visually to the whole city of Montreal. O'Donnell's chief problem here was that the fourth church of Notre-Dame would not be so advantageously situated as its predecessor. In 1672 Place d'Armes was the heart of the city, accessible from every direction. But in 1685 a fifteen-foot-high palisade was erected on the borders of the settlement.[18] Between 1721 and 1725 the palisade was replaced by twenty-foot-high stone walls with fourteen quadrangular bastions.[19] One bastion sealed off Place d'Armes from the countryside to the west, and the only gate in the west wall was about one hundred yards away. After the British conquest of 1760, the population tended to move out of the city in a line corresponding to this gate (now Saint-Laurent Boulevard). By the 1820's, when the walls had been demolished, the pattern of settlement had changed from north-south streets parallel with Notre-Dame to east-west streets perpendicular to it. As a result some citizens lived in densely populated blocks a mile or more from Place d'Armes, while just down the hill from the square there were acres of orchards and farms. As residents moved out, the region around Place d'Armes became increasingly commercialized.

Since Notre-Dame would be physically distant from the centre of population, O'Donnell contrived to give the church a visual dominance over the city. The two towers in his first design could be seen from every point in Montreal.

The Design of Notre-Dame

In the second plan of May 1824 the height of the towers was raised twenty feet, and the whole facade was transformed from a bland screen into a frontage three-dimensional and overwhelming in scale. The six pointed windows and doors now occupied only the lower half of the facade; the upper half bore a wholly new feature of three deep niches for statues (*Plate 23*). More important, the surface of the lower facade was penetrated by three gigantic arches nineteen feet wide and forty-seven feet high.

Where did O'Donnell get the idea for this second facade? It has a resemblance to the facade of the cathedral of Peterborough in England, but the likeness is not a strong one. Peterborough has three large recessed arches, but their relation to the rest of the facade is dissimilar to the arrangement at Notre-Dame. George and Richard Pain, Anglo-Irish architects, used an elevation based on Peterborough for their church of Holy Trinity, Cork (1832), and their design is wholly different from O'Donnell's.[20]

Much closer to Notre-Dame in time and place than Peterborough were three churches built in North America in the preceding decade: Maximillien Godefroy's First Unitarian Church in Baltimore (1817-18), Charles Bullfinch's Church of Christ in Lancaster, Massachusetts (1816), and Benjamin Henry Latrobe's St. Paul's Church in Alexandria, Virginia (1817-18). The three churches had in common the use of a triple-arched recessed portico.* The churches of Godefroy and Bullfinch were conceived as essays in Romantic Classicism, but Latrobe's building was Gothic Revival and seems most persuasively to have been the model for Notre-Dame.[21] The facade of St. Paul's is composed of five vertical and two horizontal divisions. The centre of the facade begins as a recessed portico with three pointed arches and two windows and three doors behind. The portico is approximately eight feet deep and forty feet high. Above it is a double string course, three oculi (perhaps in imitation of Peterborough) separated by pilasters and a second double string course. The two outer bays project slightly from the facade and flanks and appear to be bases for square towers.

Had St. Paul's been built the way Latrobe designed it, it would have been almost identical with Notre-Dame but on a much smaller scale. Specifically, the portico would have been deeper, and the facade would have terminated in twin towers. On July 14, 1817, Latrobe instructed the pastor of St. Paul's to make the portico deeper than the vestry wanted, for, he pointed out, "you have all the strength necessary to carry your towers and to support your front wall."[22] Comparing St. Paul's with Notre-Dame before the addition of the towers, it appears that the only real difference apart from scale is in the

---

*Henry-Russell Hitchcock, in *Architecture: Nineteenth and Twentieth Centuries*, p. 7, suggests that Godefroy's portico was derived from the *barrières* designed in Paris in the 1780's by C.-N. Ledoux. O'Donnell's design of 1821 for the Fulton Street Market also had a triple-arched recessed portico.

design of the windows on the flanks and on the facade (*Plates* 27, 28). In essentials the two exteriors are sufficiently close to make some relationship a certainty, even though there is no known connection between O'Donnell and Latrobe.[23] It is, however, significant that O'Donnell spent six weeks in the south between the presentation of his first elevation, without the portico, and the second elevation, which contained it.[24]

Apart from St. Paul's, three other American Gothic churches of that period had, or were intended to have, twin towers. These were William Strickland's St. Stephen's Church in Philadelphia (1823), Josiah Brady's St. Thomas Church in New York (1823-25), and Joseph Mangin's St. Patrick's Old Cathedral in New York (completed 1815).[25] The influence of these churches is doubtful, since the first two had octagonal towers, and the towers of the third remained as stumps. A more obvious example for O'Donnell to follow was the old church of Notre-Dame in Montreal. The old church had a single square tower about seventy feet high, on which was perched a double belfry. The original facade elevation designed by Chaussegros de Léry (1722) shows a high square tower on the right of the facade and the base for another on the left. Instead the left tower was built first and the right tower abandoned. De Léry's elevation marked the first appearance of twin towers in Quebec. Through the unexecuted design for Notre-Dame, this feature spread to many churches of Quebec in the eighteenth and nineteenth centuries.[26] O'Donnell may have suggested or he may have been told that the general shape of a twin-towered facade on his new church would continue a tradition which derived both from old Notre-Dame and from the mother church of Saint-Sulpice in Paris. It may also be significant in this context that, after the renovations of 1814, old Notre-Dame had three niches in its upper facade. This arrangement, rather than Latrobe's three oculi, was eventually duplicated in the new church.

The suggestion for the use of twin towers may have come from old Notre-Dame, but that church was not the specific model. The high, narrow towers of O'Donnell seem more like dry replicas of English Gothic. More specifically, their nearly symmetrical arrangement of oculi, bifurcated windows, and moldings reminds one of the eighteenth-century towers of Nicholas Hawksmore on Westminster Abbey. But there was another tower right in New York which was closer in style to O'Donnell's, with round corner buttresses and similarly proportioned windows and moldings. This was the short Gothic tower which Josiah Brady placed over the First African Church in New York in 1827, a year after it had been converted into a synagogue.[27] Brady and O'Donnell seem to have had a number of associations. Brady was the more sophisticated designer, but O'Donnell received the more significant commissions. Which man first devised this particular type of tower with its sleek vertical emphasis is not particularly important. O'Donnell drew his first tower elevation for Notre-Dame in 1823, lengthened it to 213 feet in 1824, and cut out one short bifurcated window some time after 1826.[28] The towers were erected only after his death, but they show a general fidelity to his designs (*Plate* 29).

The facade of Notre-Dame is interesting not because of the origin of its various elements but because of their smooth integration. O'Donnell appears to have conceived the facade in a modular system. In brief, the height of the towers is twice the height of the parapet, which is twice the height of the portico (*Plate* 24). The base to the first string course over the portico measures 52 feet. It is twice that distance (104 feet) from the base to the second string course just below the parapet and twice again as high (208 feet) to the topmost molding of the pyramids on the tower, above which is a five-foot cone.[29] The height of the facade is consequently marked off in four equal units of 52 feet. Just as the moldings register horizontal divisions, the pier buttresses register the vertical division of the facade into five bays whose widths vary within inches of 26 feet.

O'Donnell seems to have begun with a basic unit that was 52 feet high and 26 feet wide (2:1 in proportion). The facade was then planned to be 4 units high and 5 units wide. The height of the church can thus be expressed as [(4 x 52) = 208] feet and the width as [(5 x 26) = 130] feet. The total width is obtained with the addition of the three-foot projections of the corner buttresses on either side of the facade. There are a total of 14 units in the facade: 4 in each tower and 6 in the centre.

The fourteen units may be recognized in two ways. First, each is bounded horizontally by moldings and vertically by buttresses, piers, or pilasters. Secondly, each unit contains a pointed arch. Either as a window, a large niche, or a portico opening, the pointed arch appears fourteen times in the facade, once in each unit. The careful observer can calculate, even from a photograph, the exact height of any given point in the facade (*Plate* 23). This is possible because of the uniform height of twelve inches of every stone on the facade. Taking as an example a corner buttress from the base to the first string course, one counts three groups of sixteen courses, separated by four moldings: a total of fifty-two courses and therefore a height of fifty-two feet.

The uniformity in the size of the stones was primarily an economy measure which made both the quarrying and the laying of the stone faster and much cheaper. The smoothness of the chiselled stone and the interstices of just one-quarter of an inch gave O'Donnell the same flat wall areas of unvarying texture that he sought in his classical buildings. As a counter-measure O'Donnell exploited light and shadow in the portico, devised the projection and recession of planes in the niches, and made use of bold ornament in the crenellations to infuse a degree of asymmetry and irregularity into this precise geometric facade.

The flanks of the church were relatively more important in the 1820's than they are now. O'Donnell expected that both flanks could have been seen frontally, like a facade, and not obliquely as one sees them today. Until 1828 an observer could obtain a full view of the north flank by standing about three hundred feet away in the empty grounds of the Hôtel-Dieu. In that year, however, the hospital erected a three-story building along the length of Saint-Joseph Street. After 1829 the only full-length views of the north flank were in the artists' conceptions. The south flank was likewise obscured from public view by the construction of the rectory on Notre-Dame Street between the church and the Seminary. Today just five bays of the south side are visible from the Seminary gardens, and these are closed to the public.

The side walls contain nine bays in a total length of 255 feet (*Plate 25*). Six bays are an average of 28 feet wide and 61 feet high from the base to the eaves. Each has a pointed window 10 feet wide and 36 feet high. Three bays at the front, back, and centre are somewhat narrower and project slightly forward from the plane of the others. The first bay is the side of the tower on Notre-Dame Street, the centre bay carries a dormer with a blind window, and the last bay supports a short, square tower with a similar blind window. The lower elevation of the nine bays is identical except for the door in the centre bay. The units are divided by octagonal wall-buttresses which taper off in sixteen-foot sections to the eaves, above which they rise an additional 24 feet as pinnacles.

Since O'Donnell had not even planned buttresses in his first elevation, it is conceivable that these were added primarily for their visual effect. Engineers found in 1961 and 1962 that there was only slight lateral pressure exerted on the walls.[30] Curiously, O'Donnell had the buttresses hollowed out to serve as ducts for the hot air furnaces in the basement. The furnaces were never installed, but the idea may have influenced Bishop John Henry Hopkins, who suggested the same thing in his *Essay on Gothic Architecture* (1836).[31] Hopkins lived at that time in nearby Burlington, Vermont.

The special problem of the north wall was the fifteen-foot drop in elevation. O'Donnell's first intention was to accentuate the slope by erecting a terrace which would be level with Place d'Armes. He specified coursed rubble stone for the base of the wall on the assumption that the terrace would eventually hide it from view. The agreeable impression of brutalism which the modern observer may see in the base was thus quite contrary to O'Donnell's taste, since such rough handling of stone did not win popularity with Gothic Revival architects until later in the century.

From the north-east corner of the church one can still view the building as a total complex in design, rather than as the sum of four autonomous walls (*Plate* 30). The east wall, for example, combines elements already found in the flanks and in the facade. Its end towers are miniature versions of the front towers; the crow-step gable and blind windows recall the dormers on the flanks. From this point, where one is able to see simultaneously the east and north walls and the back of the west facade, one can appreciate the variety of shapes and angles in the design.

Three of the four walls of Notre-Dame remain today almost exactly as the architect planned them, and yet the rationale behind the whole exterior design must elude the modern observer. The role of the church as a pivotal element in the urban setting of Montreal is utterly destroyed. Even when viewed from close up, the walls of the church cannot be seen as they were intended. The flanks must be seen at an angle, and the east wall is marred by the addition of a huge chapel. When Place d'Armes was only an open space, the off-centre placing of the facade was not so obvious. But the awkwardness of the relationship was emphasized at mid-century by the creation of a raised island in the square and was accentuated even more in 1895 by the addition of the Maisonneuve statue as a point of focus.

The visual relationship of the church to the whole city has been destroyed. The vast size of the east window was designed not only for interior illumination, but also for its impressiveness to visitors in the harbour (*Plate* 34). The portico arches, which may seem unnecessarily grandiose to the observer on Place d'Armes, were also intended to be seen from half a mile away on Sherbrooke Street (*Plate* 33). So long as no tall building was placed on the west side of Place d'Armes, the complete facade was visible from the newly fashionable western heights of the city. This full view existed until 1845, when the *Fabrique* itself sold the west side of the square to the Bank of Montreal for the erection of a large office building.[32] It is not too much to suppose that the architect, who even in his will bequeathed plans for "the improvement of the area around the New Catholic Church," would have advised the wardens never to sell that plot of land in order to preserve the monumental character of his design.

THE BUILDING OF NOTRE-DAME passed through five stages: the planning and clearance of the site, and the laying of the foundation in 1823 and 1824; erection of the exterior walls in 1825 and 1826; erection of the interior structure in 1827; completion of the ceiling and part of the woodwork in 1828; and the painting and decoration in 1829.

O'Donnell directed the project both as architect and superintendent of construction. He had four chief foremen: a master stonecutter, John Redpath; a master mason, Gabriel Lamontagne; a master carpenter, Daniel Bent, replaced by Mr. Thompson and later by Jacob Cox; and a master blacksmith, Mr. Fellow. Approximately two hundred and fifty workers were engaged on the project at peak periods each summer. Some worked without pay either as volunteers or as members of work crews sent by the Militia. Most of the paid workers were farmhands who came in from the surrounding countryside before and after harvests. The least skilled of these were the labourers, who transported stone, erected the scaffolding, and hoisted materials up the walls. They were paid 2s. 6d. or the equivalent of fifty cents a day.* The masons, timber workers and joiners were paid 5s. or a dollar a day. The labourers were a constant source of annoyance for O'Donnell, who once observed:

> The Canadian workman smokes his pipe, sings his song, pulls and hurls, piles stone upon stone, towering to the clouds, without solidarity or a justness of proportion and knows not the cause that combines them. Generations must pass away before your workmen can produce one mechanic until there are [sic] a change. . . . The Canadian workmen are a noble race of men, and if they were

*The cost of a ground floor pew at Notre-Dame was £15 or $60 a year. A labourer would thus have had to work 120 days to rent a good pew in the church.

43

well trained at the proper time they would do wonders, but they are sadly
neglected — unfortunate men, I feel for them! (Letter to the building committee, April 2, 1827.)

More of a liability than the low quality of workmanship in Montreal was
the primitive state of its industry. The economy of the city depended on the
export of furs and agricultural produce. In return manufactured articles were
imported from England and the United States. Very little was produced at
home. For the construction of Notre-Dame all materials except stone had to
be brought into the city: building wood from Upper Canada; decorative
woods from Quebec City; glass, iron, and nails from England; and sand and
lime from various locations downriver on the St. Lawrence.

During the course of construction, O'Donnell had the added responsibility
of preparing detailed estimates of the amount of materials and labour needed
for each building season. From these estimates, prepared in the autumn of
each year, we can learn the approximate state of the construction of the
church.

The negotiations for a continuous supply of materials constituted one of
the significant commercial exploits of early nineteenth-century Canada. They
involved agents in Quebec, Boston, New York, and London, all of whom
communicated with François-Antoine LaRocque in Montreal. Occasionally
tenders for materials wanted would be printed and distributed in the form of
broadsides; more often they were published in local and foreign newspapers.
The first such public tender, published in the *Montreal Gazette*, June 12, 1824,
reads:

> Tenders for the Cartage to Town from the
> Quarries in rear of it, of from
> 25 to 30 M Cubic Feet of Stone,
> to be used in the Foundation of the New Catholic Parish Church of this City,
> will be received at the Office of the Fabrique, on the Place d'Armes, until the
> 18th inst. at 5 o'clock P.M.
> The cartage to commence beginning of the following week, and to continue
> without intermission until the Contract be completed, in such manner that the
> works may not be delayed. The Tenders to specify the rate per foot cube.
>
> Montreal, 8th June, 1824.[1]

The two materials which required the greatest attention were stone and
wood. Cut limestone was taken from the quarries of "Mile-End," a district
about one and one-half miles west of Notre-Dame where stonecutting flour-
ished until the 1890's. The stone was supplied to O'Donnell's specifications by
two partnerships: John Redpath and Thomas McKay, Scottish immigrant
canal-builders; and Ben Schiller and Paul l'Africain, local stonecutters. It was

then carted in mule trains to the lower town and stored on Place d'Armes and on Place Viger, about a quarter of a mile away from Place d'Armes.

Pine, fir, cedar, and oak were cut from forests around what is now Williamsburg, Ontario. The largest logs of yellow pine measured forty-six feet in length and twenty-seven inches in diameter. These were presumably cut during the winter in order to cushion their fall on snowbanks, which were piled up to twelve feet high.[2] They were then loaded as squared timbers on rafts and floated down the St. Lawrence and through the new Lachine canal in order to circumvent the rapids just upriver from Montreal. From the canal the rafts passed a few hundred yards across the harbour to the docks at the foot of Saint-Joseph Street. There long ox-carts were backed into the water on sloping platforms alongside the rafts in order to pick up the materials. Some 40,000 pieces of timber in 131 separate sizes were ordered in a single tender printed in October 1824.[3] In general the columns and upright members of Notre-Dame were of yellow pine because it grows straight and tall with few branches. The lathes of the ceiling were of cedar, the floors of white oak, and the scaffolding of red spruce.

The construction of Notre-Dame began in May 1824 with the demolition of four houses and a cemetery on the site. Workmen destroyed a cluster of passages and sacristies east of the old church and constructed a high wooden fence around the building area. When they began to dig the foundations, they found that bedrock lay about thirty feet below ground and that the earth on the site was rather soft and infiltrated by underground springs. The presence of water theatened the whole stability of the church. O'Donnell first had a deep well dug at the east end to drain off water and then placed a "crib" or grid of logs about ten feet below the intended depth of the foundations.[4] The intention was to provide a strong and uniform base to protect the walls against uneven settlement.

The nine-foot-high walls of the foundation were laid during July and August of 1824. Montreal limestone was used for these walls, as well as throughout the building. It is a hard blue-grey stone, relatively expensive to cut, but very durable. The cut stones were set in beds of mortar one-quarter of an inch thick. Earlier Quebec builders had used a random-rubble method of laying stones (*colombage pierrotté*) which incorporated great quantities of mortar. Such walls were often weakened by the crumbling of mortar in the winter.[5] O'Donnell was consequently very scrupulous in his instructions to the master mason to lock the stones together with a minimum of mortar.[6] The pointed joints of Notre-Dame have in fact weathered well and have not required a major renovation except on the facade.

On September 1, 1824, the cornerstone of Notre-Dame was laid at the east end of the church, on top of the hammer-dressed base. The ceremony brought together the élite and the masses of Montreal and Quebec City, and the proceedings took on a quasi-legendary cast in later years, as exemplified by this excerpt from *Le National* in 1876:

> Concerning the laying of the cornerstone of the building, we shall say that the ceremony had attracted an immense crowd of onlookers and passersby. The enthusiasm was so great that after a speech in which Mr. O'Donnell set forth the design of the new church and the appearance it was to take, the mob, in ecstasy, forced the worthy to sit on the enormous block which was about to be set in place with equipment for that purpose.
>
> Then with the aid of windlasses which were worked by strapping big fellows, architect and granite were lifted up into the air and, while both turned slowly in space, the crowd, impassioned and delirious, applauded and cheered "hurrah," "bravo," and "vivat," enough to snap the cables. Fortunately these held fast, and for at least ten minutes Mr. O'Donnell was the object of an ovation which his dead colleague Michelangelo had never received in his lifetime.[7]

O'Donnell's hopes for the successful completion of his project were probably never more sanguine than on that day. He spent the autumn preparing plans and estimates for Notre-Dame and then returned to New York until March.

The erection of the walls began in mid-April 1825, after the celebration of a special High Mass for the success of construction.[8] The first year there was a sufficient supply of workmen, materials, and money so that work proceeded rapidly. Ten courses of cut stone were laid on all four walls from May to July 1825. The walls throughout were composed of two or two and one-half feet of coursed rubble inside, bonded outside with two and one-half feet of cut stone. The building committee had intended to economize by leaving the south and east walls in rough-dressed stone, but O'Donnell proceeded to make them all of uniform quality.[9] In all, twenty courses of stone were laid in 1825, the remaining forty-one courses in 1826. No brick was used at any point in construction, probably because, at that time, it would deteriorate in the Canadian winter.[10]

The church was simply a shell during these years, since neither the floor nor the galleries were erected until 1827. Scaffolding covered the interior and exterior walls and was anchored to the stone by means of iron rings, some of which are still visible at ten-foot intervals on the side walls and at six-foot intervals on the facade.

O'Donnell spent the winter of 1825-26 in New York, reasonably satisfied with the progress of the work, and then returned in the spring. The building season of 1826 was again satisfactory: by October the walls had been raised their total height, the portico built, and sixteen stone piers erected in the basement to carry the wooden columns.[11] In September 1826 O'Donnell submitted his annual estimate for the forthcoming year, in which it appears that emphasis had shifted from stone to wood, since six times more labour was required of carpenters than masons:

> 52672 feet of cut stone.
> 66754 cube feet of building stone.
> about the same quantity of lime and sand wanted as used this year.
> about 1400 days mason work.
> 17000 days labour work.
> and about 1000 dollars worth of scaffolding wanted to complete the outside of mason work.
> 40792 superficial feet of roofing to be covered with tin.
> 1000 feet of sheet copper 20 of an inch thick for gutters.
> 12 leaders 5½ inch diameter and 62 feet in length [for heating ducts inside the buttresses].
> 7471 yards of plastering on laths.
> 4500 yards of *ditto* on stone walls.
> about 9000 days carpenters work and about 7000 dollars worth of materials.
> Glass and painting not included in this statement.
> (Letter from O'Donnell to the building committee, September 19, 1826.)

Normally all the workers were dismissed between October and April every year, and the architect spent the winter in New York. But O'Donnell ordered construction to continue during the winter of 1826-27 and he stayed in Montreal to direct it. In the autumn of 1826 the sixteen nave columns were set up on their stone piers. These trunks, forty-six feet high, were probably raised with the aid of a primitive hoisting device called a "gin-pole," and were erected from east to west. As each pair of columns went up, it was connected by tie beams and held together by wooden joints and iron clamps. Then the galleries were raised section by section and swung into place. The laying of the floorboards was also intricate because the floor was not level but sloped three feet from east to west. To allow the columns, galleries, and tie-beams to settle and lock together with a minimum of pressure, O'Donnell postponed the laying of the roof until later in the year. Unhappily the church was open to the sky during the near-legendary blizzard of January 1827, in which four feet of snow fell in four days and drifts gathered ten and twelve feet around and probably inside the building.[12]

The roof is the finest engineering achievement in the construction of Notre-Dame, and it is one of the landmarks in building history in Canada. The total interior width of Notre-Dame is 121 feet, 8 inches. The interior is divided into a nave 67 feet wide and two side aisles, each 27 feet, 4 inches wide. The barrel vault of the nave thus spanned a greater distance than in any other building then standing in North America (*Plates* 35, 36). Designing in the

Construction and
Decoration

Georgian tradition, O'Donnell erected a pitched roof consisting of right-angled triangles over the side aisles and a king post roof over the nave. The upper portion of the roof is 215 feet long and consists of seven tie beams which are supported by pairs of free-standing columns in the nave at a height of 80 feet above the floor. From the centre of the tie beams king posts rise to the apex of the roof, 111 feet, 4 inches above the floor. Seven principal rafters on each side link the king posts with the nave columns and the exterior buttresses on the flank walls. There are also seven intermediate tie beams, king posts, and rafters which are connected with the principal members by purloins and diagonal struts and braces. With this arrangement O'Donnell was able to concentrate the weight of the roof on the nave columns rather than on the side walls. Each column bears a vertical load estimated at ninety thousand pounds.[13] Once the framework of the roof was up, late in 1827, the rafters were covered with approximately three thousand boards which were faced with tinned iron plates (*fer blanc d'étain*) from England. Until the tin was replaced by copper in 1872, the roof of Notre-Dame glittered brilliantly in the sunlight and provided a beacon for travellers approaching the city.

Once the roof was in place, work began on the ceiling. Approximately eighteen thousand boards were used to create the barrel vault over the nave and the fan vaults over the side aisles. The interior ceiling was plastered over and prepared for painting in 1828 (*Plate* 37).

The raising of the columns, the galleries, and a roof of such immense size in less than a year was a remarkable feat. The master carpenter, Jacob Cox, tried to take credit for the achievement because he had assumed more and more authority after 1826 as O'Donnell's health rapidly declined.[14] But Cox was not an engineer, and his memoranda to the building committee show how dependent he was on the architect for all plans. O'Donnell seems to have been a most capable engineer. Lewis Willcocks wrote to the building committee, April 28, 1824, that in New York "he is spoken of by men of Science as well as practical mechanics as a very honorable mechanic of great talents in his line."

No original drawings for the roof have survived, but there is a fascinating study for the centering of the east window. It was thirty-two feet wide and twice as high (*Plate* 38). In the design O'Donnell shows the same preference as in the roof for mortise-and-tenon joints to connect as many as five pieces of wood and fasten them with pegs and iron clamps.

Engineers examined the entire structure of Notre-Dame in 1961 and 1962 and found it, with one exception, to be in excellent condition. The exception was the presence of dry rot in the nave columns. They were replaced by reinforced concrete and recovered with their original wooden colonnettes. The change cannot be detected from inside the nave. Some timbers in the attic

48

were also strengthened with steel plates. At the same time soundings were taken of the stone piers which indicated that they were solidly supported by the wooden "crib" buried in the soft ground. Considering that Notre-Dame is so large a building and that it was erected so quickly without advanced equipment, it appears that O'Donnell had an excellent grasp of engineering problems. He solved them not by radical innovations but by his meticulous and even sacrificial devotion to detail.

After 1827 the emphasis of the building campaign shifted from construction to decoration. During 1827 the wardens informed O'Donnell that they were so short of funds that neither the front towers nor the cut-stone facing of the facade could be built, but in 1828 the chief warden, Félixe Souligny, raised an additional £1,800 to pay for the completion of the facade.[15] The towers were then capped with wooden pyramids, covered with tin, and painted in imitation of stone. These would remain for fifteen years until O'Donnell's tower elevations were executed by John Ostell.

Angelo Pienovi, a Genoese painter of stage sets in New York, came to decorate the columns and ceiling in oil paints according to O'Donnell's designs. Cheap, unpainted glass was fitted into the windows, and the local painter John Doherty began to plaster and whitewash the interior walls, and to paint the doors and woodwork as they were set in place. Carpenters and masons were discharged, and joiners were hired to construct the pews, the pulpit, the gallery railings, and the choir stalls. Most of these furnishings were in mahogany and black walnut, imported through an intermediary in Quebec. In order to economize, all the confessionals and the high altar were brought in from the old church. In October O'Donnell prepared 243 separate drawings for a retable which would be placed behind the high altar. An open competition was held for the execution of O'Donnell's design, and the winner was Paul Rollin, who delivered the finished piece in 1830, too late for the opening of the church.

Of the 243 original designs for the retable, 33 still exist. They give an impression of O'Donnell's taste and ability in interior decoration. Leafing through these drawings, one feels the spirit of their designer as a Rococo plasterworker *manqué*, creating lush and frivolous forms in contrast to the general restraint of his larger compositions (*Plates* 17, 39, 40). The retable was designed as the transition between the high altar of the old church and the east window. The old altar was made in 1814 by the atelier of Louis-Amable Quevillon in a provincial Rococo style. It was shaped like a sarcophagus (*en forme de tombeau*) and was three and one-half feet high and ten feet long. Its preservation was probably a sentimental gesture, and in fact it is still preserved as the side altar of Saint-Amable. O'Donnell also had to incorporate a crude statue of the Virgin Mary (without Child) which Rollin had

49

made for the old church in 1812. The clergy added further stipulations by requesting a general similarity in plan with the altar of the mother church of Saint-Sulpice in Paris.

O'Donnell's solution was to copy, probably from Blondel's *Architecture Française,* the plan of the altar of Saint-Sulpice and its oval platform. The centre portion of the retable was made to fit the old altar, and the sides were extended so that the pinnacles were exactly aligned with the outermost mullions of the east window. In elevation the retable was forty-two feet high from the base to the cross. A niche, eight feet wide and twelve feet high, was enframed by an ogee arch and flanked by six pinnacles.* The form of the niche and pinnacles may owe its general shape to an illustration published by John Milner, but the profusion of cresting, annulets, and drop tracery is typical of O'Donnell.[16] The retable was too small to serve as the focus for such a large interior space and especially inadequate as a shade from the glare of the east window. But the ogee arch and drop tracery made an indelible impression on Quebec architects and sculptors. O'Donnell's design was repeated many times in stone and wood in the province. One of the more elaborate copies is still in place as the retable of the parish church of Saint-Sulpice, a village twenty miles east of Montreal.

O'Donnell seems to have made only limited use of architectural hand-books in creating the decoration of Notre-Dame. The pulpit and gallery railings were ornamented with a pattern of three superimposed narrow ovals which was probably copied from plate XX of Batty Langley's *Gothic Architecture, Improved by Rules and Proportions,* London, 1742 (*Plate* 42). The plan and profile of the columns also follow various illustrations from Langley. Although wildly inaccurate as Gothic designs, these plates showed step-by-step how to create "Gothick" forms in wood. They would have been of much greater help to O'Donnell than the more scholarly compendia by Rickman, Carter, and Britton, whose views of Gothic cathedrals were not intended as models for reproduction and certainly not for reproduction in wood. An American architect of the early nineteenth century could not hope to design in the Gothic Revival without using models drawn from pattern books. John Henry Hopkins acknowledged the aid of Milner's *Treatise on the Ecclesiastical Architecture of England* (1811) and of John Britton's *Cathedral Antiquities of Great Britain* (1814-35) in designing Trinity Church, Pittsburgh, in 1823.[17] The more sophisticated French architect Maximillien Godefroy depended on Peter Nicholson's well-known *Principles of Architecture* (1795-98) in creating Gothic forms for the chapel of St. Mary's Seminary in Baltimore in 1806-7.[18] Benjamin Henry Latrobe also studied Gothic forms in Brit-

*Thomas Rickman used a similar design for his large gateway to the New Court of St. John's College, Cambridge (1825-31).

ton and sent a copy to his pupil Robert Mills.[19] Still, Latrobe indicated his annoyance with the deficiencies of such pattern books when he wrote: "... I am obliged as to the Baltimore Cathedral to design from memory. I cannot here procure a single *technical* account or representation of a Gothic Building of any superior merit; but the style, & even the detail is so impressed on my imagination that I hope to succeed in escaping the censure you so justly bestow on Wyatt. ..."[20]

In 1823 there was only one book of Gothic designs which could have substantially helped O'Donnell to decorate Notre-Dame. That book was *Specimens of Gothic Architecture* (1821–23) by Augustus Charles Pugin, and it was both archeologically correct and easy to reproduce. There is no evidence however, that O'Donnell actually used it, probably because his conception of Gothic was one of plaster and wood, and not of stone. A delightfully incongruous bit of "Gothick" is his freehand rendering of the finial which crowned the retable. Like some overripe acanthus leaf from the pages of Stuart and Revett, the finial suggests a taste for sensuous form and rich shapes which the architect curbed almost until the end of his life (*Plate* 41).

In December 1828 Paul Rollin and his associates began to carve the retable, choir stalls, gallery railing, and pulpit according to the designs of O'Donnell. W. H. Bartlett's steel engraving of *c.* 1838 shows choir stalls which are much like their present successors, with the exception of brattishing on top and two thrones at either end of the horseshoe (*Plate* 16). It was customary throughout the nineteenth century for all the Sulpician priests to fill these stalls at High Mass. Many contemporary reports cited the pulpit as a copy of one in the Cathedral of Strasbourg, and there is enough resemblance to suggest that O'Donnell must have followed an engraved view as his model. Bartlett represented the congregation sitting in box pews which enabled them to turn about to listen to the preacher instead of facing the altar. Other drawings and later photographs show that worshippers, except for the wardens, sat in slip pews facing east; the wardens sat in the pew of honour facing the pulpit on the north. Their special pew, the *banc d'oeuvre*, had its own nine-foot long altar on which were placed a silvered crucifix and two candelabra. These objects were traditionally described as gifts of Louis XIV and are still on view in the church museum. After vespers the priests would walk around the *banc d'oeuvre* and the altar with their censers. In 1859 Bishop Bourget forced the termination of this custom and had the altar, which was felt to bestow too much prestige on the wardens, removed.[21]

The interior of Notre-Dame was rushed to completion in the spring of 1829. As a temporary measure the gold and green Corinthian baldachin of the old church was placed behind the high altar (*Plates* 14, 15). The church was opened for services without pews on the feast of the Pentecost, June 7,

51

1829, by Jean-Henri-Auguste Roux, Superior of the Séminaire de Saint-Sulpice and titular Curé of Notre-Dame. When the pews had been installed, the
church was blessed in a four-hour ceremony on July 15, 1829. (Consecration
according to full canonical regulations took place only on May 19, 1929.)[22]
Since Bishop Plessis of Quebec had died in 1825, Auxiliary Bishop Lartigue
was invited, as a gesture of reconciliation, to celebrate the inaugural Mass.[23]

The architect, the president of the building committee, and the head of the
Seminary died within two years of the completion of the church. O'Donnell
died the following January, Curé LeSaulnier a week later, and M. Roux a year
after that.

Destruction of the old church of Notre-Dame began early in 1830 and was
complete by November. Its contents were scattered, and only the bell-tower
remained on Place d'Armes until 1843.*

On September 16, 1832, the building committee terminated a decade of
activity. François-Antoine LaRocque reported that exclusive of land, construction of the church had cost £47,446 (approximately 15 per cent over
the estimate). Of this sum, about £8,000 had been given from the resources
of the *Fabrique*, £7,000 in donations from the public, £10,000 in interest-free
loans from the Seminary, and approximately £22,000 had been borrowed at
6 per cent interest. The money was spent in the following approximate
amounts: £3,000 on iron, £4,000 on wood, £18,000 on stone, £2,000 on
other materials, and £20,000 on salaries.[24] The minutes of the wardens' meeting continue:

> Mr. LaRocque then requested for himself and for the other members of the
> Building Committee that the said Committee now be discharged. Upon which
> it was RESOLVED that this Board is perfectly satisfied with the work of the
> said Building Committee. It thanks all its members, those who are wardens as
> much as those who are not, for the zeal, the care and the industry which they
> have shown in having the new church built. And ratifying all in this qualifica-
> tion and to this end, they have made them a full and complete discharge.[25]

---

*Charles Dickens observed in 1842: "There is a very large Catholic cathedral here, recently
erected; with two large spires, of which one is yet unfinished. In the open space in front of this
edifice stands a solitary, grim-looking square brick tower, which has a quaint and remarkable
appearance, and which the wiseacres of the place have consequently determined to pull down
immediately." (Charles Dickens, *American Notes*, pp. 239-40.)

SINCE NOTRE-DAME was opened for worship in 1829, it has been the subject of a vast amount of critical analysis. This analysis has been of two types. The first, which began in the 1830's and which still can be read today, concerned itself primarily with the design and function of the church. The second and more popular type began in the 1860's, but became quite common only in the twentieth century. This analysis concentrates on the style of Notre-Dame and examines above all the relevance of the Gothic Revival to French Canada. The first type of reaction will be discussed here, the second in Chapter IX.

From 1823 to 1829 there were many published accounts of the progress of work at Notre-Dame, particularly on the exhibition of O'Donnell's first plan in October 1823, the laying of the cornerstone in September 1824, and the opening in July 1829. These accounts describe the church, but tell very little about the feelings, pro and con, which Montrealers must have had towards the new Notre-Dame. The first writer who departed from conventional terms of praise for the church and who wrote, in 1841, a thorough critique on it was the French architect Pierre-Louis Morin.[1] There is, however, another gauge of public opinion on Notre-Dame during the years of its construction and that is the regard for James O'Donnell. O'Donnell obviously made a great impression on Montrealers. A French-language journalist in 1876 linked his name with that of Michelangelo, and even as late as 1897 an English writer called him "a fit companion of Christopher Wren."[2] Such posthumous acclaim confirms that O'Donnell was held in great esteem by both the French and English-speaking communities of Montreal in the 1820's. In his will, written after just five years' residence in the city, O'Donnell mentioned as friends or executors a founder, a president, and a vice-president of the Bank of Montreal as well as three prominent financiers, two distinguished physicians, and a future justice of Lower Canada.

O'Donnell's popularity was reflected in the commissions he received. Even before he decided to settle in Montreal, he was offered a commission to build a "House of Industry" for the Governor of the Quebec colony, the Earl of Dalhousie.[3] Again in 1827 the Governor asked O'Donnell to come to Quebec City to submit certain unspecified plans, but pressure of work on Notre-Dame prevented him from going.[4] In December 1824, six months after O'Donnell had settled in Montreal, the American Presbyterian Congregation chose one of his plans for their new church at the north-west corner of Saint-Jacques Street at Place Victoria (*Plate 53*). The congregation included many wealthy merchants from Boston and New York. Mindful of their American ties, O'Donnell had composed a design which was based on two illustrations in Asher Benjamin's *The American Builder's Companion*.[5] The two-story cut limestone facade had a centre projection of three bays, capped by a pediment and designed to carry a tower.* The three doors flanked by panelled pilasters and surmounted by recessed arches show an obvious derivation from Benjamin's Old West Church (1806) in Boston. O'Donnell built in limestone instead of brick, inserted a fanlight over the centre door, and added Gothic detail to the side doors and to the five tall windows on the flanks. The unexecuted tower would have had a stone base with volutes, as in another Benjamin design, plus an open two-story wooden spire which resembled O'Donnell's work in Rochester. When the church opened in December 1826, the interior was simply and tastefully decorated, with graceful Ionic columns supporting a curved gallery and a sumptuous mahogany pulpit before a niche and four Ionic columns on the back wall.

The surviving records of the American Presbyterian Congregation do not specify the architect of this design, but the visual and circumstantial evidence points overwhelmingly to O'Donnell. Although O'Donnell spent his first three winters in New York, the minutes of the building committee, December 7, 1824, show that he was in Montreal on December 6, 1824, when the congregation selected its plan. Not only was O'Donnell a distinguished visiting architect from New York, he was a close acquaintance of Horatio Gates, the chief vestryman of the American Presbyterian. Gates, the Boston-born president of the Bank of Montreal, was first involved with O'Donnell as chief commissioner of the Montreal House of Industry in 1824. In 1825 he was paid £25 by the wardens of Notre-Dame to inspect the architect's plans and

*The intended elevation of the church is seen in a water colour by John Drake, 1826, plate XV of the "Album de Jacques Viger," Archives du Séminaire de Québec, Quebec. There are two interior views in the Notman Photographic Archives, McCord Museum, McGill University.

estimates for their church.[6] In 1826, Gates, as president of the British and Canadian School, accepted O'Donnell's designs for a new school building. It was also Gates who made the final choice of a plan for the American Presbyterian in December 1824.[7] Not only the Gothicized design of the church but even its stonework suggests the participation of O'Donnell. The lower string course on the side wall of the church alternates with the lintels of the basement windows. At O'Donnell's British and Canadian School there is an analogous effect in the string course which also serves to form the sills of the second-story windows.

The British and Canadian School at the north-east corner of Côté and de Lagauchetière Streets is the second building still standing in Montreal that may be attributed without doubt to O'Donnell (*Plate 54*). Now used as a bakery and much disfigured, the school was originally two stories high and seven bays long, with an octagonal cupola over a hipped roof. It was used by 275 pupils, although it was claimed that over 600 could be accommodated.[8] Constructed of plain limestone and decorated with quoins and with corner blocks in the architraves of the windows, the school demonstrates O'Donnell's typical practicality and conscientiousness in that all the rooms received ample illumination and the construction was massive and durable. O'Donnell donated the plans for the school in 1826 as a way of becoming acquainted with the leaders of Montreal society. The patron of the school was the Earl of Dalhousie, the president was Horatio Gates, and the members included François-Antoine LaRocque and representatives of the Papineau, Viger, and other influential families.

O'Donnell might have built other works in Montreal. Certainly he would have had numerous other commissions had he lived beyond 1830. Even these two buildings suggest what influence O'Donnell had. The American Presbyterian Church was deliberately *retardataire*, but it was still the first effort to free Montreal architecture from the monotonous blocks which were erected until the 1840's and 1850's. Its mixture of Georgian and Gothic effects on the exterior was common two decades earlier in the United States, but still very rare in Canada. Even the British and Canadian School was avant-garde since its panelled architraves were the earliest precursors of the Greek Revival in Montreal and conceivably in all of Canada. The four most productive architects of the mid-nineteenth century in Montreal, Victor Bourgeau, Pierre-Louis Morin, John Ostell, and John Wells showed in their works definitive traces of the influence of O'Donnell, despite the fact that he died four or five years before any of them came to practise in Montreal.

It is instructive to turn for a moment from his works to the character of James O'Donnell. His only known writings consist of his will and twenty-one letters which he sent to the building committee of Notre-Dame. Most of the letters confine themselves solely to matters of construction, but a few contain impressions or other thoughts. The following two excerpts concern O'Donnel's theories on the regulation of society. Discussing New York he wrote:

> This is a place where our leisure hours can be employed in more amusement than in Montreal, it is true there are more advantages in New York and the state of society are more happy, and more suited for moral enjoyment. In well regulated society here that studied reservedness are not known, man are only estimated by his worth and moral rectitude, his own self-importance are not the standard by which he is rated, he must be useful and bear a respectable com-[panion?] through life. And those of the higher gifted mind might with an acute sensability and impeachable deportment hold their station in the scale of human dignity. (Letter to the building committee, January 20, 1826. Original spelling and punctuation.)

In another letter O'Donnell contended that much better organization was required at Notre-Dame and digressed upon the role of science in history:

> Man in his rude state composes a part of the great machine of nature and it only wants superior judgment to put him in motion and to make him useful to himself and to his fellow man. Science bursts the chains of stupidity and gives boundless scope to thought which creates an unlimited spirit for emulation.
> It is useless, to repeat, for any person who are unskilled in these matters to contend with me on the method of carrying on work to advantage with out system. I can adduce inexhaustible evidence: the Works of Creation alone proves it, as God him self is the author of System. His infinite Works and the perfection of their periodical movements is a School even for the Divine, the philosopher and the Mathematic to contemplate on their systematical movements, the more they contemplate the more they admire until thought is lost in boundless space. (Letter to the building committee, April 3, 1827.)

The letters portray O'Donnell as a complex personality: aggressive, condescending, and proud of his professional status. O'Donnell enjoyed making a grand gesture, as he did in one letter of April 2, 1827, to the building committee which began: "Gentlemen, The crisis has arrived." But his patrician bearing held a measure of petty tyranny which was demonstrated in the humiliating twenty conditions of submission which he forced on the head mason, Gabriel Lamontagne in April 1827. O'Donnell was also sensitive, suspicious, and in his last years, distinctly paranoid. He invariably turned against one colleague after another. Through the years 1826 and 1827, for example, he bestowed extravagant praise on the carpenter Jacob Cox. By May 1828 he was equivocal: "Enduce the carpenters to work with more spirit and more study if possible." In September 1828 O'Donnell complained publicly of Cox and even after the completion of Notre-Dame in August 1829, he attacked

Cox for insubordination. In one of his last pathetic letters, O'Donnell made the charge that workmen had stolen his detailed drawings.

O'Donnell worked himself to death on Notre-Dame. He liked to speak of the project as his martyrdom: "I have been a slave to the building since its commencement," he wrote. There were other dark references to a race with death for completion of the project. As early as 1823 he noted lugubriously that plans would be ready "if I am spared," and the same observation appeared frequently thereafter. For some years O'Donnell had suffered from edema, but it had not totally incapacitated him. As soon as he became idle in July 1829, however, his condition rapidly deteriorated.

On November 14, 1829, O'Donnell dictated his will.[9] A prime concern was that all his architectural plans be published by the "Royal Society of Arts" in Dublin. In fact no society by that name ever existed in Dublin, and no public collection in Ireland today has any record of such a large group of O'Donnell drawings. O'Donnell carefully allotted £8 6s. 8d. each to the Catholic, Anglican, and Presbyterian poor of Montreal. Two maps of the Place d'Armes area and an elevation of a tower for Mount Royal were bequeathed to the Natural History Society of Montreal, but they were never delivered. Salary and interest still owed him by the church were paid to his executors and presumably forwarded to his three married sisters in County Donegal. O'Donnell and his estate received a total of £3,724 from the *Fabrique* up to 1837. His annual salary of £375 was quite modest compared, for example, to the £600 per annum the Bank of Montreal paid in those years to its head cashier.[10]

On the day he drew up his will, O'Donnell also prepared for death by converting to the Roman Catholic faith. The conversion caused great excitement in Montreal and was even reported in a two-page account in *The Jesuit,* a Boston newspaper. The ceremony of conversion apparently took place in the presence of a large crowd,

> before whom he candidly declared it was not the solicitation of friends or others, neither could it be any worldly interest, but the conviction of his own heart that induced him to abjure heresy and make an open profession of the Roman Catholic faith. . . . This unshaken faith and firm confidence manifested by floods of tears on the day that he received the Holy *Viaticum,* inspired the assistants with fervour and devotion even to tears (S. N., *The Jesuit,* pp. 202-3).

Even today there is a widespread belief, kept alive by Montreal journalists, that it was his involvement with Gothic architecture which led O'Donnell to the Catholic church. Such whimsical thinking is refuted by the hypothesis of the nineteenth-century Sulpician historian Pierre Rousseau. The seminarians had apparently attempted without success to convert O'Donnell during his final illness. "Mr. Quiblier, to overcome the last reluctance of O'Donnell, would have offered that he be buried in the church — This would have resolved the conversion in scenes of emotion."[11]

O'Donnell died less than three hundred feet from the church, at the home of Dr. Loedel, about 2:00 P.M. on Thursday, January 28, 1830, "still invoking the holy name of *Jesus, Jesus, Jesus*."[12] He was given an imposing funeral, and his body was entombed in the crypt of the church. The wardens had a marble tablet affixed to the tomb so that today the only marked grave in Notre-Dame is that of O'Donnell.[13] The following memorial tribute appeared in the *Montreal Gazette*, February 4, 1830.

Died

On Thursday morning last, Mr. James O'Donnell, Architect, aged 56. In announcing the death of this gentleman, we should be very deficient in our duty were we not to notice the high professional talents for which Mr. O'D. was distinguished. The new Parish Church of this city, were other specimens of his skill wanting, would be enough to stamp his name as a first rate Architect, but his portfolios were replete with designs, which, on many occasions, had obtained for him premiums from celebrated foreign institutions. Those who had the pleasure of his intimate acquaintance, will appreciate the loss which the community of Montreal has sustained in Mr. O'Donnell, whose mind was constantly bent in reference to the improvement of this city, where he had fixed his residence for several years past. His private character was such as to endear him to all with whom he associated; his modest unassuming deportment, and his truly amiable disposition, procured him many friends, while his high professional attainments will cause the city of Montreal long to regret the loss of so eminent an artist. He bore the severe malady under which he laboured with exemplary patience, and at last sunk into the arms of death, with becoming resignation and fortitude. His remains were on Monday morning interred in the vaults of the Cathedral — a splendid monument of his talents, and well worthy of his fame.

Although early descriptions are rare, by the middle of the nineteenth century scores of visitors had written upon Notre-Dame. The church was in fact second only to Niagara Falls as the leading tourist attraction in Canada. Reading through these descriptions, it is apparent that three aesthetic judgements predominate. The first and by far the most common opinion was that the size of the church was extraordinary and the facade in good taste, but that the interior was a disappointment. Thus, as an example, James Silk Buckingham wrote a meticulous three-page description of Notre-Dame in 1843 which concluded: "While the exterior of the building is imposing from its size, and chaste in its simplicity, the interior is more awkwardly arranged than any similar edifice I remember."[14]

The astonishment of travellers at the size of Notre-Dame was based not only on its physical dimensions but also on a comparison with the backwardness of Montreal and Canada at the time. As one local resident described Montreal:

> The city was composed of one and two story houses, very few of three stories, built with very few exceptions of rubble stone, plastered over. All the stores and many of the houses had iron doors and shutters; many buildings had vaulted cellars, and many had the garret floored with heavy logs, covered with several inches of earth, and flat paving stones, with a stone stair-case outside, so that a roof might burn without doing further damage.[15]

Everything about Notre-Dame marked a first in the history of building in Canada. It was the highest building, it had the widest clear span, and it encompassed the greatest interior volume of any construction in Canada. The audacity of having erected such a monument appealed to the pride of Canadians even much later in the century. *La Minerve*, in 1866, emphasized with satisfaction "the enormous structure of the towers, which no one has dared to build for almost three hundred years in the Christian world."[16] Even foreign visitors wrote that Notre-Dame was surpassed in size only by the largest of the medieval cathedrals of France or by St. Peter's.[17] At mid-century it was still called the largest building, religious or secular, in the New World.[18] Certainly it was the largest church in Canada or the United States until the completion of St. Patrick's Cathedral in New York in 1879. Even then Notre-Dame could seat four times as many worshippers as could St. Patrick's.

Unlike St. Patrick's, Notre-Dame did not take thirty years to construct. The church was built in a race against Mgr. Lartigue's cathedral of Saint-Jacques. Construction and decoration of Notre-Dame required just four and one-half building seasons, or a total of thirty-five months. The lack of money was equally acute. Notre-Dame cost less to construct than some of the cheapest buildings of the 1820's, the "Commissioners' Churches" in England. The cost of these churches was calculated to average no more than £8 a head.[19] O'Donnell built his church for under £5 a head, that is, £47,000 to seat ten thousand worshippers.

The second attitude, encountered much more rarely, found the exterior adequate, but lavished even greater praise on the interior. So B. W. A. Sleigh wrote in 1846:

> The Roman Catholic Cathedral is the largest in America, and the turrets can be seen towering over the city. Its interior decorations are very costly, and the high altar, after St. Peter's at Rome, is as fine a thing as could be seen in Europe. . . .

When I first entered the Cathedral, the solemn tone of the organ at Vespers, the choristers' chants, the candles burning on the numerous altars, refulgent with gold and costly gems, the sombre and subdued light, reflected in a thousand prismatic colours from the stained windows, and mellowed by the rays of the setting sun, while the gentle tones of female voices, the Nuns of the Hotel Dieu and Soeurs Grises (Grey Sisters) pouring forth from their hidden shrines strains of sweet melody, in concert with the fine voices of the monks, filled me with a religious awe, and impressed me with the grandeur of the scene.[20]

The third attitude, encountered about as commonly as the second, concentrated its attention on the defects of the interior. The following excerpt is from a long article that appeared in *La Revue Canadienne* in 1845:

From that point where Montreal becomes visible there can also be discerned the towers of our magnificent church. In approaching it, one cannot help admiring its impressive proportions, its style of architecture which is as simple, austere and solemn as the roman religion. But how great is the disappointment upon crossing the threshold. You expect the interior of a cathedral to be as somber, awesome and imposing as the idea of God who resides therein. Instead, it is something hazy, dull, cold, unfinished; on the ceiling a motley daubing of blues and greys, without poetry and without taste, on the walls numerous dirty streaks, long cracks, stains of rain and moisture.[21]

Many critics could not understand how so splendid a building could appear so shabby inside. Actually the interior was not so much shabby as incomplete. The ceiling and columns were not finished as intended, the elaborate pattern of wooden tracery was left off the vaults, cheap, painted glass rather than stained glass was placed in the east window, and for a decade the pulpit even lacked a staircase.[22] Still worse, the hot air furnaces were never installed in the basement so that eight wood-burning stoves were placed in the side aisles and blackened the walls with soot.

Surprisingly, forty-five years passed before the wardens took any step to ameliorate the interior, so that even in 1875 local residents complained of the "black and mildewed walls of this expansive, but gloomy and unfinished edifice, without the least adornment."[23] The wardens, however, were more sensitive to outside opinion — especially the opinion of foreigners and Montreal Protestants — than they were to the needs of the parishioners. The first major improvement to Notre-Dame was the completion of the western towers in 1841 and 1843. This project was directed by John Ostell, an architect who had come to Montreal from London in 1834, and he faithfully executed O'Donnell's elevations. The desire for exterior magnificence induced the wardens to spend approximately twenty thousand dollars during the 1840's to purchase bells which would ring out over all Montreal. The largest bell, it was claimed, could be heard twenty-one miles from Montreal, on Mont Saint-Hilaire.[24] To complete the facade, the Italian sculptor Baccerini was commissioned in 1864 to make artificial stone statues of St. Joseph, St. John the Baptist, and the Virgin Mary (patron saints of the country, the province, and the city) for the large niches above the portico.[25]

Before they could turn to the embellishment of the interior, the wardens had to pay for the building of a dozen new churches in the expanding parish of Montreal. The cost of operating the cemetery of Notre-Dame-des-Neiges as well as such imposing churches as St. Patrick's, St. Anne's, and Notre-Dame-de-Grâce almost brought the mother church of Notre-Dame to financial collapse. In 1866 the subdivision of the parish of Montreal was finally decreed by Rome. For half a century the Sulpicians and the wardens of Notre-Dame had staved off this decree, but now the loss in spiritual authority was in part assuaged by their release from a crushing financial burden. After 1866 the Sulpicians and the wardens had only the church of Notre-Dame as their responsibility.[26]

Some of the critics of Notre-Dame realized that the project had run out of money in 1829 and that the interior had remained substantially unchanged since then. Others, such as Captain J. E. Alexander, made more imaginative attempts to explain the exterior-interior dichotomy: "I then visited the cathedral, a most magnificent Gothic pile of recent erection; but its tawdry internal decoration, its blue compartments and spotted pillars, caused the death of the unfortunate architect, who died of a broken heart, disgusted at the bad taste which had spoiled his handiwork."[27] Foreigners often passed over the main lines of the interior without comment, but severely criticized the gaudiness of the painted decoration.[28]

The considerable diversity of opinion on Notre-Dame hinged mainly on the origins of the observers. There were approximately ten published accounts of Notre-Dame by French-Canadian writers up to 1870. About half of these criticized the church interior on the grounds that certain features discomforted the worshippers. Again and again, their principal attack was directed at the darkness of the nave in contrast to the brilliant and even blinding light of the east window.[29] Foreigners who came to Notre-Dame not to pray but merely to observe often took totally opposite views of the interior. It was exactly this contrast of light and dark which so pleased B. W. A. Sleigh in the passage previously quoted. The interior also excited another writer who was much less given to romanticism than Sleigh, Henry David Thoreau:

> Coming from the hurrahing mob and the rattling carriages, we pushed aside the listed door of this church, and found ourselves instantly in an atmosphere which might be sacred to thought and religion, if one had any. . . . I did not mind the pictures nor the candles, whether tallow or tin. Those of the former

which I looked at appeared tawdry. It matters little to me whether the pictures are by a neophyte of the Algonquin or the Italian tribe. But I was impressed by the quiet religious atmosphere of the place. It was a great cave in the midst of a city; and what were the altars and the tinsel but the sparkling stalactics [*sic*], into which you entered in a moment, and where the still atmosphere and the sombre light disposed to serious and profitable thought?[30]

In general, visitors who shared O'Donnell's Anglo-American background had the highest praise for the interior. Perhaps the extreme contrast of darkness and light brought to mind passages from Edmund Burke's *Philosophical Inquiry into the Origin of Our Ideas of the Sublime and Beautiful*. In his influential book Burke had written: "I think then, that all edifices calculated to produce an idea of the sublime ought rather to be dark and gloomy," and "A quick transition from light to darkness, or from darkness to light, has yet a greater effect. But darkness is more productive of sublime ideas than light."[31] Another English visitor who represented the interior of Notre-Dame as sublime was W. H. Bartlett. Like Thoreau, his view of the church was one of a great cave with light cutting through the gloom (*Plate* 16).

It seems that O'Donnell's taste was ahead of his time in his preference for darkness over the Georgian tradition of light. Twelve years after Notre-Dame was designed, John Henry Hopkins wrote: "There is no fault more common, and none more opposed by every principle of good taste, than having too many windows in Churches."[32] Hopkins went on to cite Sir Thomas More's *Utopia* in which More says that temples should be dark not from poor design but from the choice of their priests, " 'because immoderate light scatters the thoughts'." O'Donnell was also progressive rather than old-fashioned in his choice of intense, contrasting colours for Notre-Dame rather than white — the usual colour in Georgian churches.

To sum up the many opinions of nineteenth-century critics on Notre-Dame, one could say that the great majority liked the exterior, but were divided in their opinions on the interior. A small group of Canadian critics thought it should be redecorated, while a somewhat smaller group of foreigners considered the interior the best part of the design. There were other miscellaneous opinions. Some critics were amused by the theatre-like arrangement of Notre-Dame. Some, like the American novelist William Dean Howells, spoke of the starkness of the interior with irony: "It has something of the barnlike intensity and impressiveness of St. Peter's."[33] Among the most perceptive of the critics were those who recognized Notre-Dame for what it was: one of the largest and most convenient meeting halls of the nineteenth century. Its qualities of acoustics and visibility were especially appreciated by the men who had preached there:

The Church of Notre-Dame, provided with huge galleries arranged in steps, is certainly the most colossal auditorium in Christendom. . . . It appears moreover that this gigantic covered space is marvellously resonant, and that without exertion, without shouting, one is heard everywhere. And it is a delightful sensation, which I do not think one could experience elsewhere, to speak quietly with ten thousand souls.[34]

Although O'Donnell was unable to complete the decoration of Notre-Dame, he fully discharged his main duty of providing space to seat ten thousand people in relative comfort. If there is any lasting judgement on Notre-Dame, it must acknowledge the fact that the church is one of the very few buildings erected in the early nineteenth century in America that still performs its original function.

𝔙ictor 𝔅ourgeau
and ℜotre-𝔇ame CHAPTER VIII

𝔄s one sees it today, the church of Notre-Dame is the creation of two architects, James O'Donnell and Victor Bourgeau. For the average visitor the facade, appearing exactly as O'Donnell conceived it in 1824, is far less impressive than the interior, which was redecorated in the 1870's by Bourgeau. This redecoration has a history which is in many ways similar to the history of the original construction. First there were complaints of the inadequacy of the interior, followed by pressure on the wardens to improve conditions; eventually, a general plan of action was determined, and an architect selected. But there were also differences. This time the Curé of Notre-Dame was not an onlooker but the driving force behind the work. And the model for emulation was no longer the current fashion in London and New York but the newly-recognized splendour of medieval Paris.

The subdivision of the parish of Notre-Dame de Montréal was effected in 1866, at a time when it covered fifty-five square miles and served eighty thousand parishioners in over a dozen branch churches.[1] Now, concentrating their energies on a single parish of approximately five thousand members, the seminarians saw that a complete renovation was necessary to restore Notre-Dame to its position of supremacy in Montreal. The subdivision of the parish had also entailed the appointment of a new curé for the church. The position went to Benjamin-Victor Rousselot, a Frenchman from Angers, who held office from 1866 to 1882. He immediately pledged himself to reconstruct the interior of Notre-Dame.[2] Within a month of his appointment, he began to raise money; by the end of his first year in office Rousselot and Etienne-Michel Faillon, another French priest, had determined the main lines which the renovation should follow.

65

Victor Bourgeau and Notre-Dame

Faillon was an able historian and amateur architect who had lived for a time in Montreal and then had rejoined the Sulpicians in Paris. In his correspondence with Rousselot, Faillon made clear that the renovation should be based not only on practical considerations but also on aesthetics and even symbolism. He pointed out to Rousselot in a letter of April 9, 1867, that the east window of Notre-Dame was not simply an impractical means of lighting the nave, but that it was inappropriate as well, for he claimed that in no church or cathedral in France was one designed for this purpose. Instead of a flat altar wall with a window, Notre-Dame should have a semicircular apse and, if possible, rose windows should be inserted into the ceiling.

A number of plans embodying such changes were submitted to the wardens between 1866 and 1869, including those of four architects, François-Xavier Berlinguet of Quebec, Patrick C. Keely of Brooklyn, August Sawyer of Ottawa, and Napoléon Bourassa of Montreal; all suggested that more light be admitted by suppressing one of the galleries and adding a clerestory or by inserting openings at various points in the ceiling.[3] All but one of the plans were self-conscious imitations of French Gothic, with a semicircular apse, an ambulatory, and even radiating chapels. The addition of these protuberances behind the altar and the construction of cupolas and lanterns in the vault would have destroyed the structural and decorative integrity of Notre-Dame. Rousselot seems to have realized this, for in 1869 he requested the plan of a more modest and harmonious scheme of improvements from still another architect, Victor Bourgeau.

Bourgeau was the most active and one of the most imaginative architects in nineteenth-century Quebec.[4] His career in architecture spanned almost sixty years and included forty years of involvement with Notre-Dame. Among his extant works are four great monuments in Montreal: the huge complexes of the Hôtel-Dieu, the convent of the Grey Nuns, the interior of Notre-Dame, and the exterior of the third church of Saint-Jacques. Bourgeau was born on October 26, 1809, in the village of Lavaltrie, Quebec. He was trained as a wheelwright by his father, but he had so little education that he was unable even to sign his name on his marriage contract. About 1830 Bourgeau happened to meet an Italian painter (presumably Angelo Pienovi of Notre-Dame) who induced him to read Vignola. Bourgeau then became a sculptor, a contractor, and finally an architect. His first recorded work was the wooden staircase for the pulpit of Notre-Dame in 1844.

Bourgeau's first building was the church of Saint-Pierre-Apôtre in Montreal, 1851. It was commissioned by the *Fabrique* of Notre-Dame, and the result was in a sense a critique by Bourgeau, showing how he would improve on O'Donnell's church. At Saint-Pierre he erected a single central tower projecting from the facade, and side walls with buttresses and pinnacles set in bold relief. Inside, the proportions are more vertical than at Notre-Dame, and there is a deep horseshoe apse instead of a flat east wall, with two balconies over the entrance which jut out at angles rather than in the semicircle employed by O'Donnell. There are no side galleries. Saint-Pierre thus appears in its main lines and in much of its decoration to be a miniature Notre-Dame, but it is executed with a richer play of forms and under the influence of French Gothic.

Just four years later Bourgeau was invited by the wardens to submit plans for the renovation of the interior and exterior of Notre-Dame. These plans were followed by a wooden model of the interior in January 1857.[5] In February the Curé accepted Bourgeau's plan for renovating the choir. The architect then left to study churches in France and Italy in preparation for his neo-Gothic work for the *Fabrique*, and a neo-Baroque cathedral for the Bishop of Montreal.[6]

Of this first group of Bourgeau proposals, submitted between 1855 and 1858, there survives only an elevation of the exterior.[7] This is a scheme to erect a semicircular apse of seven bays so well integrated that the whole of the exterior would appear to follow a single design. On his return from Europe Bourgeau extended the organ loft of Notre-Dame by twenty feet to give it its present appearance. This was a relatively minor work, necessitated by the purchase of a new organ. The overall plan of reconstruction was abandoned until the appointment of Curé Rousselot in 1866. Bourgeau himself was now more intrigued by the Baroque than the Gothic style. For the nuns of the Hôtel-Dieu in Montreal and the Ursulines in Trois-Rivières he could build in the Baroque style, but rural parishes generally insisted on something Gothic. For them Bourgeau would build a hybrid, like his church at Saint-Barthélémi, a transposition of Notre-Dame into round-headed arches (*Plate* 52). He erected twenty-two churches in Quebec and in the United States and counselled on the decoration of twenty-three more. In many of these projects some aspect of Notre-Dame was almost certain to appear.

In 1869 Bourgeau returned to the problem of Notre-Dame and presented to the new Curé and wardens a plan which was less grandiloquent but far more practical than his earlier ideas or those of his rivals (*Plate* 44). His proposal, submitted with the nominal participation of his partner Alcibiade Leprohon, sought to replace the patchwork of side altars with just two designs: one for the four altars flanking the side doors and one for the two altars at the east end of the side aisles. The problem of light would be solved by inserting lanterns between the ceiling and the roof without actually modifying the form of the vault. Bourgeau wanted to create a new high altar, but the choir stalls of O'Donnell were to remain untouched. O'Donnell's retable would be replaced by one quite similar, but slightly wider and much taller.

Victor Bourgeau and Notre-Dame

On either side three new niches were to be placed in the same style to surmount the curve of the choir stalls. The bare expanse of the altar wall, one of the least attractive aspects of O'Donnell's design, would be covered by projections which would act as giant archivolts to the window. The hoped-for effect of these changes would be to create the semblance of an apse, even though the church would still terminate in a flat wall.

The wardens approved this plan and commissioned Bourgeau to begin by placing four skylights in the vault.[8] But the wardens of 1869, unlike those of 1823, were no longer in command. Bourgeau's plan pleased them because of its simplicity and economy, but Curé Rousselot apparently considered it inadequate because it did not block off the east window. He postponed all work until 1872, when he returned from a trip to France and Italy. While in Paris, Rousselot was impressed by the appropriateness of the Sainte-Chapelle as a model for the interior of Notre-Dame, both in style and symbolism.[9] He evidently used his visit to commission ten large statues from Henri Bouriché, an old friend from Angers then resident in Paris.

The insertion of four skylights proceeded slowly from 1872 to 1875. First the pitch of the roof was raised to ward off snow, and the tin covering was changed to copper. Skylights were cut into the roof, and octagonal drums were set in the attic below. From the inside one can see only three octagonal "rose windows" over the nave and a strip of glass over the sanctuary. By June 1874 Bourgeau had also executed new gallery railings and capitals; then work came to a halt during two years of financial depression.

In 1876 Bourgeau initiated the second phase of the project in a speech to the wardens on his new plan of decoration.[10] Essentially his program for the sanctuary was to frame the ten large statues in white pine which Rousselot had commissioned in Paris in 1872 and which had arrived in Montreal the preceding summer.[11] Bourgeau's solution was to erect a reredos almost eighty feet high which would accommodate the statues and replace the east window as the centre of attraction inside Notre-Dame. First O'Donnell's window was blocked off and plastered over. Next projections were built up from the wall in accordance with the elevation of 1869. The choir stalls were replaced by very similar seats in mahogany, and six statue niches were placed above them.

The reredos had to follow the iconographic program devised by Rousselot in 1872. The theme was the Holy Eucharist, its prefiguration in the Old Testament and its fulfilment in the Crucifixion.[12] Copying the form of O'Donnell's retable, consisting of a niche capped by two pinnacles and a large finial, Bourgeau in effect made a huge enlargement which corresponded to the height and width of the suppressed window (*Plate* 45). The iconography begins with Bouriché's relief of "The Institution of the Eucharist" on the face of the altar. In the large niche above the altar is the Crucifixion, representing the physical sacrifice of Christ which is perpetuated in the Eucharist. Around the Crucifixion are four Old Testament prefigurations. In the lower right niche Abraham is about to sacrifice Isaac (Gen. 23). At upper right, a priest of the house of Aaron sacrifices a lamb (laws of sacrifice, Lev. 16: 22). In the upper left niche Moses places an omer of manna in the vessels of the holy Ark (Exod. 16: 33, but the officiant should be Aaron and not Moses). At lower left Melchisedek, king and high priest of Salem, greets Abraham with bread and wine (Gen. 14: 18).[13]

The uppermost niche of the reredos shows the "Coronation of the Virgin," a group which Bouriché seems to have modelled after the stone carvings in the porch over the central door of the cathedral of Rheims. Bourgeau's three upper niches also seem to derive from the porch of Rheims, although the spires and pinnacles over them were more likely chosen in homage to the Sainte-Chapelle. The reredos rests on a shelf cantilevered out from the east wall and is supported by iron tie rods anchored at the back. Its effectiveness stems mainly from the contrast of the light-coloured statues with the dark background and the ample spacing of each statue within its niche. It appears that the six polychrome plaster statues of St. Peter, St. Paul, and the four Evangelists were made for some other purpose and then mounted on high pedestals.[14] In relation to the nave, Bourgeau's work has the scale and impressiveness which O'Donnell's retable never achieved.

It is apparent from his reluctance to destroy the east window and his retention of so much of the original design in the sanctuary that Bourgeau saw himself as the restorer and not the destroyer of O'Donnell's conception of Notre-Dame. Bourgeau was in fact responsible for a partial resurrection of one of O'Donnell's designs that had been abandoned before 1829. It will be recalled that O'Donnell had proposed an elaborate network of applied tracery to give the ceiling the appearance of ribbed vaulting (*Plate* 19). Instead, for almost fifty years the ceiling was simply painted in alternating stripes of blue and grey. The ceiling pattern executed in 1876 by Bourgeau and a M. Cleff was not as intricate as O'Donnell had proposed, but it restored fan vaults in the side aisles and designated five ribs to radiate across the nave from each column. The new plan also accommodated the three octagonal skylights and added an ancient Quebec (and European) motif of gold stars on a blue-green sky.

Where he thought more emphasis was called for, Bourgeau did not hesitate to cut into the fabric of O'Donnell's church. In order to make the sanctuary a more dominant focus for the nave, Bourgeau changed the widths of the nave bays which O'Donnell had established. He began by suppressing the blind arch of the first bay on the east, so that it is now the only bay without transverse penetrations. Bourgeau understood that O'Donnell had intended the sanctuary to function as a stage and so he accentuated the second bay by adding more colonnettes to the columns and thickening the transverse ribs overhead. The entrance to the sanctuary was thereby transformed into the equivalent of a proscenium arch. Bourgeau also followed O'Donnell in his preference for strong colour. In 1828 O'Donnell indicated that the nave should be painted red, yellow, brown, and blue.[15] Bourgeau had the nave repainted in silver, gold, blue, azure, red, and purple.[16] The influence of the restored Sainte-Chapelle was also apparent in his taste for polychromy and in specific details such as the diagonal banding of the columns.

The completion of the sanctuary in 1880 left a few projects still unrealized before Notre-Dame assumed its present appearance. Bourgeau was involved in all but one of these. During the 1870's the interior walls of Notre-Dame were given wainscotting to a height of six feet above the floor and confessionals and side chapels were set in place. Six of the chapels followed the two designs shown in Bourgeau's elevation of 1869. In 1886 the wardens ordered a massive new organ from Les Frères Cassavant of Saint-Hyacinthe, Quebec. Bourgeau designed a framework of eight cast-iron columns to support the weight of its six thousand pipes. It is likely that he personally designed the arrangement of the pipes to fill the void between the organ loft and the ceiling and to create a shimmering backdrop for the nave (*Plate* 47).

In his last work, the pulpit or *La Chaire de Verité*, Bourgeau achieved the most perfect example of that combination of Gothic and Baroque which extended the life of the Gothic Revival in Quebec from the arrival of O'Donnell to the end of the century. The basic design of the pulpit was made by Bourgeau in 1872 and modified to include the present staircase sometime before 1888.[17] The pulpit rests against and even entwines itself about the forty-six-foot height of the middle column on the north side of the nave (*Plate* 48). It begins as a sinuous, free-form staircase to the preacher's box. Tucked into the cavity of the staircase are pine statues of Ezechiel and Jeremiah by Louis-Philippe Hébert. Hébert's miniature statues of Old Testament prophets and Christian saints fill the niches of the speaker's platform. Overhead, Baroque cherubim support the octagonal sounding board. Over the canopy stand St. Basil, St. John Chrysostom, St. Augustine, and St. Leo. These figures in turn support an allegorical statue of the Christian Knight. Bourgeau, himself a sculptor, encouraged Hébert to realize in this pulpit one of the finest creations in the last flowering of traditional Quebec wood carving.[18]

Victor Bourgeau died on March 1, 1888, before the renovation of Notre-Dame was complete. In 1884 Pierre-Louis Morin supervised the addition of a baptistry in the shape of an elongated octagon with a domical vault. In 1889 Henri-Maurice Perrault and Albert Mesnard (the first a nephew of John Ostell, the second a pupil of Bourgeau) erected the large sacristy in an English Gothic style with a superb open timber roof. In 1888 the new curé Léon-Alfred Sentenne commissioned them to design La Chapelle du Sacré-Coeur directly to the east of the original church. Thirty years after Victor Bourgeau tried to make Notre-Dame more French with the addition of the *rond-point* (apse), his successors fortified its Englishness by tacking on what was in effect a Lady Chapel. The chapel is entered through the east wall of the original church, directly below the blocked window. It is ninety feet long, eighty-five feet wide at the transept, and fifty-five feet high. It is a curious building, not a Latin cross in plan but T-shaped, and it has four stages in elevation: a nave arcade, a gallery, a blind clerestory and an open clerestory. Within the chapel one may detect Greek columns, Roman arches, Baroque staircases, Moorish galleries, and Indian, Persian and Gothic decoration (*Plate* 49). Sacré-Coeur is remarkable only for its ornate wood-carving.

About 1892 O'Donnell's troublesome east window was given a reprieve. After fifteen years some of the plaster was removed and the iron sheathing dismantled so that worshippers could look through glass from the mother church to its effusive offspring.[19] The architects presumably anticipated this opening since they made the ceiling supports in the chapel in the identical shape and position of the east window. Perhaps Perrault and Mesnard were inspired by the use of glass in Les Invalides, but their creation was far less edifying than its prototype. The window was blocked off for the last time in 1898 and painted over with a fine sunburst.[20]

While the east window was open, one could have seen simultaneously three versions of the Gothic Revival in Quebec: O'Donnell's (1820's), Bourgeau's (1870's), and Perrault and Mesnard's (1890's). Of the three, it was Bourgeau who was most successful in expressing the architectural taste of the province of Quebec. He had opened the way to flamboyance in Quebec architecture but, unlike his imitators, he had acquired self-restraint from his knowledge of the monuments of Europe and from his early experience as a craftsman. From the 1850's to the First World War the Bourgeau style was the archetype of Quebec church architecture and decoration. For the last forty years of his life, between designing the staircases for the pulpits of 1844 and 1888, the renovation of Notre-Dame was Bourgeau's prime concern. During those years he brought into the nave light, colour, and a wealth of forms. O'Donnell created a potentially exciting interior for Notre-Dame, but it was Victor Bourgeau who brought it to life.

Victor Bourgeau and Notre-Dame

𝕿HE LATE MONSEIGNEUR OLIVIER MAURAULT described Notre-Dame in 1929 as "a truly national monument, where the religious and patriotic sentiment of French Canadians expresses itself with incomparable brilliance."[1] More common today is the idea that Notre-Dame is incongruous or totally alien to the spirit of Quebec. This opinion was originally formulated by the two scholars who led the revival of interest in Quebec architecture. In 1947 Ramsay Traquair wrote in *The Old Architecture of Quebec* (p. 2): "In 1824 Notre-Dame de Montréal was rebuilt in a bastard American Gothic. This was the first great blow to the old French tradition; it died hard, even today traces of it can be found, but we may close our history in the mid-nineteenth century."

He was supported in 1949 by Quebec's leading architectural historian, Gérard Morisset: "the Irish Protestant James O'Donnell of New York . . . ignores our whole tradition and climate. And what is this Gothic style which the architect imposes arbitrarily on the new Notre-Dame? It is a 'troubadour' Gothic of English origin, cut and dry forms, shabby moldings and irrational construction."[2]

The second generation of Canadian art historians then took different sides in the argument. Alan Gowans wrote that Notre-Dame had garnered popularity among French Canadians because they liked the French and Catholic connotations of the Gothic style.[3] Robert Hubbard countered that Notre-Dame had actually displeased the French Canadians because they considered it too English and Protestant.[4]

The problem is not how Notre-Dame appears today in relation to Quebec but how French Canadians saw it in the 1820's and later in the century. Notre-

Notre-Dame as a French-Canadian Church

Dame was the first Gothic building of importance to be erected in the province and in all of Canada. But as Gowans suggests, there is evidence that Notre-Dame was meant not to destroy but to perpetuate certain aspects of the traditional Quebec style of architecture. It became the most influential building in the architectural history of Quebec because it was acknowledged that the traditional style was no longer adequate. Contemporary reports hardly ever recognized Gothic as being a foreign style, and the general public never considered Notre-Dame in terms of hidden implications, either English or French, Protestant or Catholic.

The history of the Gothic Revival in Quebec begins only in 1823, but there is an earlier prehistory. A good example of earlier knowledge of Gothic in Quebec is provided by Joseph-Octave Plessis, Bishop of Quebec from 1808 to 1825. His knowledge and appreciation of Gothic are of interest not only as typical opinions of an educated Quebec clergyman but because Plessis, through his voluminous correspondence with M. Roux of the Séminaire de Saint-Sulpice in Montreal, may have affected the style of Notre-Dame. Plessis left a diary of his trip to Europe from 1819 to 1820. On page after page of this diary he gave intelligent, succinct, and enthusiastic accounts of the Gothic churches he visited: Southwell and Westminster Abbey, Canterbury, and Notre-Dame in Paris.[5] He showed a definite preference for Gothic, revealed in his severe criticism of the dryness of St. Paul's in London and in his greater delight in seeing the Cathedral of Milan than St. Peter's.[6] Interestingly, Plessis also found England much more to his liking than France.[7]

Plessis also appreciated the Gothic Revival and particularly liked a church which was well known to James O'Donnell and to some of the wardens of Notre-Dame, St. Patrick's Old Cathedral in New York:

the interior is magnificent. Six high clustered columns on each side divide the whole body of the building into three naves surmounted by Gothic arches, forming an impression still more imposing because a painter has represented on the end wall of the church, behind the altar, a continuation of those arches and columns which seem to fade off in the distance and create such a strong illusion to visitors who have not been warned that they at first imagine the altar to be only at mid-point in the length of the church, although it actually touches the end wall. The great effect of its perspective makes the church pass for the finest in the United States. It is also remarkable for the size of its windows, for the elegance of its two galleries, one above the other, whose symmetrical staircases lead to the organ over the entrance door. The pews in the nave are arranged to allow for three wide aisles and are entirely ornamented with triangles and railings of mahogany.[8]

The Bishop of Quebec left only one recorded opinion on Notre-Dame. In a letter a month before his death he remarked that the Sulpicians of Montreal were building their church on a Gothic plan which was too large for the means of the parish.[9] It is, however, hard to conceive that the acceptance of the Gothic style in Canada was not in some way aided by Plessis. Superior Roux of the Seminary was one of his closest friends. Lewis Willcocks was an even stronger link. He was the chief warden of St. Patrick's and acted as host to Plessis in New York. He continued to see and write to Plessis until 1824.[10] Willcocks was also a friend of O'Donnell and acted as agent for Notre-Dame in New York. Although opposed to Notre-Dame for political reasons, Plessis would surely have been pleased at the idea of a great Gothic church rising in Montreal.

There were two other factors which made it easier for O'Donnell to design his new church in Gothic style. The first was the appearance of Gothic in the old church of Notre-Dame; the second was the participation of the Sulpicians in the Revival. There are three references which show that the seventeenth-century church of Notre-Dame was considered by contemporaries to have certain aspects of Gothic. Two references are only fragmentary: the young dilettante Romuald Trudeau in "Mes Tablettes," June 19, 1823, praised old Notre-Dame for "*son goût gothique*," and in 1829 a poem was printed which lamented the desertion of the old church with "*ses vitraux gothiques.*"[11] The third reference is much more substantial and intriguing. In the unpublished "Précis d'Architecture" of the Reverend Jérôme Demers (*c.* 1826) one can read:

> All contemporary architects agree that pointed rib vaults cannot be used except on Gothic ceilings. Thus it is a great oversight, to say the least, that it has been permitted to place them on the ceiling of the old parish church of Montreal. And as some of our so-called architects do not know how to distinguish between genuine beauty and abuse, it was their mistake to imagine that this ceiling constructed in one of our great cities was a model to be copied, wherefore all the rib vaults which we see, to our shame and our confusion, in a great number of our newly-decorated churches.[12]

It should not be surprising that the Messieurs of Saint-Sulpice would have Gothic decoration in the form of windows and ribs in their favourite church. The four most important priests of the Seminary — Curé LeSaulnier, the Superior Roux, his successor Quiblier, and M. Roque, the head of the college — were all born in France and had returned occasionally both to the continent and to England. It is unlikely that these men, some of them graduates of the Sorbonne, would be any less informed about Gothic and the Gothic Revival than Bishop Plessis, who until 1819 had never seen Europe. Nor can one ignore the fact that the first building in the New World which could legitimately be called Gothic Revival was the chapel of the Sulpician Seminary of

St. Mary's in Baltimore. Both the Montreal and Baltimore seminaries were directed by refugees from the French Revolution and visits between them were frequent.[13] Although the building of Notre-Dame was in the control of the lay wardens and not the priests, the previous acquaintance of the Sulpicians with the Gothic Revival certainly aided in the acceptance of O'Donnell's plan.

It thus appears that the wardens were not wholly surprised when O'Donnell made his proposal that their church be the first Gothic building in Canada. The Bishop knew and liked the style, the Seminarians were acquainted with it, and there was already a touch of Gothic in old Notre-Dame. But there is no evidence whatever that the wardens actually told O'Donnell to design in the Gothic style. O'Donnell was unknown to them until he entered their employ almost by chance. O'Donnell was a Gothic enthusiast, but they were not. They wanted their church to be cheap and functional. As LaRocque said to an architect who had pointed out that Gothic churches must be based on a Latin cross plan: "I think that we shall stick with the Gothic in the form of a rectangle which has advantages that, it seems to us, are not equalled by those which are offered by the cruciform."[14] O'Donnell probably approached the wardens with the same argument that Benjamin Henry Latrobe had used unsuccessfully with Bishop Carroll of Baltimore in 1805: the Gothic style costs no more than the classical but gives a church more splendour for the money.[15] The patrons of Notre-Dame were not conservative prelates but self-made businessmen; the very novelty of erecting Canada's first Gothic building may have appealed to them.

There was novelty in the new Notre-Dame, but there was also a continuation of the old. The idea of twin towers was most likely suggested by de Léry's partially executed elevation of 1722. The three niches in the upper portion of the facade may correspond to the two similar niches and a window on the old church facade. Inside, the shape of the sanctuary, its reverse-curve railing, the position of the choir stalls, and the altar were surely modelled after the same arrangement in old Notre-Dame. The old church had only one side gallery, but there were two balconies over the entrance. The organ lofts of both churches exactly correspond in that they had horseshoe-shaped projections and pews arranged in the form of an amphitheatre.[16] The names of the five chapels in the old church reappeared in the new, and three altars even occupied an equivalent position within the new nave.[17]

It appears that all parties immediately concerned with the building of Notre-Dame were quite satisfied with the Gothic style. Among the general public there was an overwhelming (but not unanimous) approval of Gothic architecture. Thus when the second Bishop of Montreal, Mgr. Ignace Bourget, studied a niche which contained a venerated statue of the Virgin in the

Cathedral of Chartres, it naturally reminded him of the retable in the parish church of Montreal.[18] From the 1830's to the 1860's magazines such as *Mélanges Religieux*, *La Bibliothèque Canadienne*, *La Revue Canadienne* and *Le Franc-Parleur* occasionally criticized the lack of decoration and light in Notre-Dame, but an attack on the Gothic style itself was very rare. Two of the latest and most sophisticated articles on the church in *La Minerve* in 1866 and *Le National* in 1876 lauded the Gothic style and Notre-Dame even though they recognized that it had been erected at a primitive stage in the Revival.

There were just two attacks on the use of Gothic at Notre-Dame. The first came in letters to the building committee from Jérôme Demers, Superior of the Seminary of Quebec and author of "Précis d'Architecture."[19] He hoped to make the "Précis" the Quebec equivalent of the texts of Vignola, Gibbs, and Blondel which he so admired, but the work was essentially just a compilation of hints and warnings to architects. Demers criticized O'Donnell's design on three points: The church should be in the classical style which was more suitable for a Catholic church; the O'Donnell plan (which Demers knew only from news reports) bore too much resemblance to a Protestant church; and the proposed church would be structurally unsound.[20] Demers implied that he could countenance a Gothic design were it at least based on a Latin cross plan. He proposed an alternative design by his protégé Thomas Baillairgé. The building committee was naturally upset at these charges and sent Demers's objections and Baillairgé's plan to O'Donnell in February 1824. O'Donnell replied on March 16, ignoring the Protestant–Catholic discussion, brushing off suggestions of structural instability, and ridiculing Baillairgé's church as being full of portholes.* The building committee was satisfied, the suggestions of Demers and Baillairgé were formally rejected, and the controversy was closed. Twelve years later, however, there appeared in *Le Canadien*, June 27, 1836, an article which was almost certainly inspired by Demers, but was supposedly quoting an anonymous visiting Italian who singled out Notre-Dame as a bad example for rural churches to copy. This time Demers's criticism provoked no response for, as the article itself pointed out, a number of churches were already following the lead of Notre-Dame in adopting Gothic.

One of the most appealing theories about Notre-Dame suggests that the wardens' commission of a Gothic church was a symbolic means of affirming their French and Catholic heritage.[21] It must, however, be recalled that the wardens did not stipulate Gothic, they merely accepted it. The one man in Quebec who thought of Gothic in terms of its symbolism was Abbé Demers and he did not praise Notre-Dame as French and Catholic, but damned it as English and Protestant. It is possible that Notre-Dame was designed to outshine the nearby Christ Church of the Anglicans, but the only conceivable

*The letter is reprinted as Appendix A.

Notre-Dame as a French-Canadian Church

"battle of styles" was with Mgr. Lartigue's cathedral of Saint-Jacques, and "style" in the 1820's in Montreal meant size and magnificence, not a period in architectural history.[22]

Far from being an exclusively racial manifestation, the construction of Notre-Dame was marked by interracial harmony and a lack of sectarianism. The architect and three of his chief assistants were Protestants, and the awarding of tenders was made in strict impartiality. Nine Protestants pledged three hundred pounds sterling as soon as construction began.[23] Eleven thousand pounds, or fully half the borrowed funds, were supplied by the Jews of Montreal during construction.[24] The church was of course intended as a monument to the glory of French Canada and its construction could, in that sense, be considered nationalistic; however, there is no solid evidence that the Gothic style was specially chosen as a vehicle for this expression.

Because Notre-Dame had not been conceived in terms of symbolism, there was no excitement when forty years after its construction, it was realized that the parish church was in large measure based on English prototypes. An article in *La Minerve* in 1866 saw no reason to disguise this fact. It emphasized Notre-Dame's affinity with English cathedrals on several points, notably in the choir, "which is in the form which one sees in all the Cathedrals in England, but which is not sufficiently ornate to produce its true effect as at York, Lincoln, Exeter, Chichester, Windsor, etc., etc."[25] Under the Frenchmen Rousselot and Faillon in the 1870's, there was a policy of redecorating Notre-Dame along French lines, but the idea of expressing one's nationalism by means of architecture gained currency in Quebec only in the twentieth century.*

For many years there has been a claim that Notre-Dame is a replica, or was at least intended as a replica, of Notre-Dame de Paris. Although this claim is still made today, there is not the slightest evidence to support it. There is no mention that the wardens ever asked for a reproduction of the church of Paris, but had they asked for it they would not have accepted such an extremely superficial likeness as one sees in the facade of O'Donnell's church. The priests and some of the wardens had visited Notre-Dame de Paris and they surely had access to engraved views of it. If they had wanted a replica of it, they would have forced O'Donnell to make one. The churches of Notre-Dame in Montreal and Paris were not even mentioned together until 1841, when Pierre-Louis Morin casually observed that the towers in Montreal were just two and one-half feet lower than those of Paris.[26] Twenty-five years later, in

*An example of this was a lecture given in 1917 by Ovide Lapalice, archivist of Notre-Dame. Lapalice stated that O'Donnell had made a thorough study of the churches of Europe, "particulièrement de la France." This was a deliberate misrepresentation of what O'Donnell had written in his letter of March 16, 1824: "except in France which I have not been in." ("Assemblée Annuelle de la Société d'Archéologie," *Le Canada*, December 22, 1917.)

La Minerve, April 28, 1866, a writer claimed only that the two churches had *"à peu près les mêmes dimensions."* None of the official guide books to Notre-Dame have ever suggested that it is a copy of the Paris church. It is mainly English Canadians who assume that Notre-Dame took both its name and style from Notre-Dame de Paris and insist on calling it a cathedral.[27]

It is somewhat misleading to speak of a Gothic Revival phase in French-Canadian architecture. There was instead a period in which the model of Notre-Dame in Montreal exerted great influence on Quebec church architecture. The English in Quebec used Gothic in their houses, their churches, their schools, their civic institutions and, with considerable success, in their office buildings. But for the French Canadians the *néo-gothique* implied only a visual refinement of an old style, hardly so fraught with literary and symbolic overtones as the Revival occasioned among the English. The French restricted their use of Gothic almost entirely to churches. Even the Sulpicians preferred the classical revival for their rectory of 1849 built beside Notre-Dame, and Bishop Bourget had his episcopal palace of the same year designed in classical form, even though the chapel inside was Gothic. The English may have been encouraged to use Gothic by the example of Notre-Dame, but after their first experiment with Gothic in O'Donnell's American Presbyterian Church, they immediately began to build fairly accurate replicas of English models.[28] Certainly they never drew inspiration from the parish church of Montreal. The French, on the other hand, had no archeological leanings for several decades and as a contemporary wrote in *Le Canadien*, June 27, 1836, they were content to build *"des imitations d'une imitation,"* that is, scale models of Notre-Dame.

Notre-Dame in Montreal was the most frequently imitated building in the province. Within eight years of its completion four Catholic churches in Quebec were built with Gothic detail. For seventy-five years Gothic was the leading style for church architecture in French Canada.[29] The three most elaborate of the Catholic churches in Gothic style — St. Patrick's, the third church of Saint-Jacques in Montreal, and the Cathedral of Trois-Rivières — all showed direct reference to Notre-Dame in the arrangement of their interiors. There were at least three outright copies of Notre-Dame, of which the most grandiose was at Sainte-Anne-de-la-Pérade. This was built from 1855 to 1869 by Casimir Coursol and incorporated some of Victor Bourgeau's suggestions for the interior renovation of Notre-Dame (*Plate 51*).

But Notre-Dame also influenced scores of churches not built in the Gothic Revival style. These are the Romanesque and Baroque churches of the latter half of the nineteenth century that reproduced only the general features of O'Donnell's design.[30] A typical example is the parish church of Saint-Barthélémi, designed by Victor Bourgeau and built in 1866-68 by Zéphirin

79

Notre-Dame as a French-Canadian Church

Perrault (*Plate 52*). As Alan Gowans first recognized and stated in *"The Baroque Revival in Québec"* (p. 12): "St. Barthélémy is an interesting stylistic phenomenon; actually, it is the 1824 Gothic facade of Notre-Dame in Montreal metamorphosed into Baroque — the same triple-arched portico, niches, twin towers and dramatic verticality, all transformed into the more 'Catholic' style."

The erection of so many churches in the Gothic style or at least in emulation of Notre-Dame seems to support the allegation that O'Donnell's church destroyed the native tradition in Quebec church architecture. But a close reading of events suggests that the old style was for all practical purposes dead a generation before O'Donnell came to Montreal. The "traditional" style of ecclesiastic architecture in French Canada was established by the six stone churches which Bishop Laval erected in the region of Quebec from 1669 to 1680.[31] The designs of these churches and their derivatives in the early eighteenth century had to take into consideration the local climate conditions, the population, and the liturgical requirements; their construction was determined by the existing methods of building and by the material available. On the exterior they had high-pitched gable roofs with graceful steeples and simple whitewashed facades and side walls. Their interiors were about twice as long as broad, with hemispherical apses and hemispherical chapels at the transept ends. Such churches were austere on the exterior but cheerful inside and generally attractive because of their fine proportions and the harmonious relation of each part to the whole.

By the second half of the eighteenth century the simple style of these churches was no longer in fashion. Both the Basilica of Quebec and the parish church of Montreal underwent successive additions and renovations. When Mgr. Lartigue planned in 1822 to build the first large new church in the colony in half a century, he accepted a design whose exterior resembled Servandoni's facade of Saint-Sulpice in Paris and whose interior even incorporated several features of the Anglican Cathedral of Quebec.[32]

As one rural parish after another rebuilt its church in Rococo opulence, two attempts were made to return to the original style of Quebec church architecture. The first was a plan which Abbé Pierre Conefroy of Boucherville designed *c.* 1790-1800 to revive the simple lines of churches of a century earlier. It served as the model for nearly one hundred churches of the early nineteenth century.[33] The other revival was a joint effort of Abbé Demers and Thomas Baillairgé to retain the plan of the seventeenth century but to improve the elevation by employing the designs of James Gibbs in such features as architraves and towers.[34]

The neo-colonial revivals instigated by Conefroy, Demers, and Baillairgé were ultimately unsuccessful because they tried to suppress rather than accommodate the increasing desire for magnificence and sumptuous decoration in Quebec church architecture. O'Donnell's Gothic Revival was compatible with the change of taste in Quebec, whereas the "native" revivals were not. O'Donnell, as a foreigner, could only suggest the direction which the new vernacular style might take. It was left to Bourgeau to fully adapt the Gothic to the native temperament, both at Notre-Dame and throughout the province. The best of the modern churches in Quebec are still those that fulfil the needs of their parishioners not only for optimum visibility and acoustics but also for richness and intimacy. With these characteristics, they carry on the pioneer efforts of O'Donnell and Bourgeau at Notre-Dame.

One thinks of Notre-Dame as a national monument of French Canada not only because of its architectural style but because of the brilliant ceremonies which have filled its nave since 1829. The most splendid was probably the funeral of Sir Georges-Etienne Cartier, the former co-Premier of Canada in 1873. Since Cartier died in London, the wardens had several months to prepare a grandiose funeral for which the church was draped in black and five hundred burning tapers were placed on an immense catafalque (*Plate 43*).[35] The most famous event that took place in Notre-Dame was not a religious ceremony but a speech delivered by the father of French-Canadian nationalism, Henri Bourassa, at the Twentieth Eucharistic Congress in 1910. The Congress was the first to be held in the New World and included such ceremonies as a Midnight Mass in Notre-Dame at which five thousand workers took communion before the altar.

The French Canadians resented the systematic suppression at that time of French-language public schools throughout English Canada, and the inflamed atmosphere of the Congress reflected this resentment. At its final meeting in Notre-Dame on September 10, Cardinal Bourne of Westminster infuriated the audience with the suggestion that the Church in Canada entirely abandon the use of French outside Quebec. Bourassa replied in a magnificent extemporaneous address which brought him international prominence. He pointed out that most of North America had been explored by French-speaking Catholics from Quebec and that three-quarters of the Catholic clergy on the continent owed their training to orders which were based in the province. Bourassa concluded with an appeal for tolerance for all nationalities within the Catholic Church. When he had finished, the great crowd inside Notre-Dame and the thousands massed in Place d'Armes went wild with indescribable delight.[36] The speech of Bourassa in Notre-Dame remains the most famous defence of the language and traditions of French Canada.

The continuing popularity of Notre-Dame manifests the intelligence with which O'Donnell and Bourgeau synthesized the desires, the resources, and the practical needs of the parish. O'Donnell first turned to the English style

Notre-Dame as a
French-Canadian
Church

which had provided churches of considerable utility, elegance, and structural soundness. He then incorporated into his plan elements which were traditional in Quebec architecture. Bourgeau later added to the interior the characteristic colour and brilliance found in the art of French Canada. Notre-Dame, as planned by O'Donnell and renovated by Bourgeau, became the model for parish churches in Quebec for seventy-five years. Its galleries, its giant reredos, its polychrome decoration, and the lines of its facade appear in scores of churches throughout the province today. Its statues, paintings, and historical scenes in stained glass encompass three centuries of religious and social expression in Quebec. Notre-Dame, the parish church of Montreal, has become the parish church of French Canada.

Letter from James O'Donnell to François-Antoine LaRocque

APPENDIX A

Dear Sir:

I have the honour to acknowledge the receipt of your friendly letter, together with the series of criticism on the sketches I made for your Church. My dear friend, I can not be silent on this occasion without expressing my grateful thanks for your gentlemanly conduct thruout, and particularly by your last communication which evidences some of the noblest qualities that can adorn the human mind, such impressions made on my mind will remain with me as a lasting monument of your worth.

I wrote to you last month answers to your former letter and would have answered your last communication on its receival had I thought the subject required it.

With regard to the remarks, they came too late to make any alteration in the plans which I am now engaged in, nor had they come before the plans I am inclined to think that I should not have made any, unless it was the express wish of the Committee, because the plans are still susceptible of any alteration that may be deemed necessary. It is time enough to make such alterations in the plans, when every thing shall be truly investigated and fully explained, if it should then be found that all those defects pointed out by the Gentleman becomes really necessary to repairs, all can be made in the working drawings where all the detailed parts will be shown by me, as the architect whom your Committee may employ.

When I had the honour to be present at the last meeting of the Committee on my leaving Montreal, I told the Gentlemen that any alterations they might deem advisable in the plans, they could have it done to their wishes, and still my plans are such as will admit of any that consists with propriety and in *accord with the principals of architecture. When I was there, before I attempted to make any sketch for your Church I examined the quarries and inquired into all the qualities of the materials, inspected the site of the Church and had been furnished with a map of the same. I also requested to know the probable sum to be expended on the erection of your Church. All this I have done in order to enable me to form such plans as would unite the whole. I then formed a few rough sketches in the Gothic style, as I considered it more suitable to your materials, workmen, climate, wants and means etc. I endeavoured to keep every thing in view, and to do the best I could for your Board yet it appears I have not succeeded in any of my attempts in the few sketches I left with the Committee.*

With respect to the remarks made on my plan, the translation does you high credit, and do honours to the Gentleman who wrote them, which shows him a man of learning, reading and observation in architecture. Many of his remarks are true, and should be adhered to by your Board.

But all those that relates to the plan and style of your Church, I consider them foreign to the subject; they are only applicable to the monuments of Europe, and to Roman architecture, not at all to the pure Gothic style, because he condemns some of the grandest and best features that art ever invented, or science had established, which shines inimitable on earth and so happily adapted to sacred use.

However, I shall not attempt to answer any of his remarks made on my sketches, though I could do it with as much truth and ease as the sun that shines, and perhaps to the satisfaction of every Gentleman in your Committee, but I deem it quite unnecessary, time will demonstrate the whole. How shall I enter into any defence relative to my professional character, although he classes me among pretenders. I will only observe that I have studied under some of the first Masters, and have carefully examined some of the best monuments in Europe, France excepted which I have not been in.

But those who may be desirous to know any thing of my character will find it before the public in the United St. as a practical architect this 12 years, and will find that I am the only architect native or foreigner admitted among the academicians in the American Academy of Fine Arts in New York. How far I am fitted to project plans and conduct your Church it is not for me to say.

I will only observe that such a plan as the Gentleman recommends to your Board, to carry it into execution, would require the materials, workmen and Coffers of Europe, and then would be as defective in point of style and convenience as the sketches which have been the subject of his remarks. Such a plan as he describes would be crowded with columns and flights of steps, occupying the apartments that rather should be alloted to the accommodation of the Congregation, and the access to the building would be laborsum, owing to the altitude of the base and besides the windows would be too numerous, and would resemble port holes more than windows suited to an Edifice of its intended magnitude and purpose. Let your Board reflect well on the plan the Gentleman describes, and see if it accords with your means and purpose in all its bearings.

As to his remarks touching strength, proportion and effect, it is but the A.B.C. of my profession and I feel as much interested for the purity of style etc. of your Church as any other, and secondly I feel for my own character as an architect and I assure you that the subject of your Edifice have occupied much of my mind since I first undertook to project plans for it.

And as to the florid style of Gothic work, it neither suits your materials, workmen, Climate nor even had you the means, the plane and simple style divested of its ornaments, comports more with the purpose of your Edifice which you will perhaps soon find out to be the case.

Bold and massey relievo with its true features in its just proportion from a palace to a cottage, produces the sublime, which those trifling decorated parts never can strike the beholder with grandure, they are the efforts of bad taste, which have degenerated from the Classic style. Classic architecture despises the busy efforts of the chisel to decorate deformity, only produces a mass of confusion subject to perish in its infancy by the corroding hand of time, particularly when exposed to the northern climates.

I am however very desirous that the Board should procure plans from other quarters as the Gentleman recommends. Paris and London are the most likely places you will succeed, of course you will incur considerable expense and detain the work another year, but then you will be better able to judge of merit and the experience will enable your Committee to determine for themselves.

I have only to request of the Board that who ever they employ to project plans for your Church, that they will not exhibit nor communicate the form nor style of my plans to them, if so it will not be treating me correctly, let them design from the sources of their own choice or copy from other edifices. And the architects plan you make choice of, employ him to carry it into execution, otherwise you will not do your selves nor him justice, as his plan and the work will be submitted to the mercy of others.

As to my self, I am not at this time much inclined to engage any further in the work if the Committee can get those that will suit better, but should they feel satisfied of my capability and agree to either of my proposals, I will still undertake to conduct the work and do the best I can for your Board. Therefore I will not engage in any other employ before the first of next month.

With regard to the plans, I will have them completed by the 10th of April *if my health is spared, and ready to your orders I shall have them bound on cards in a port folio and put up in a box or case, so as they will be secure. I have nothing more to communicate at present.*

I now must solicit your indulgence for not writing sooner and I fear that I have trespassed too much on your patience by the length of this letter, therefore I conclude hoping to hear from you soon.

I remain dear Sir, your greatful [sic] and much Obliged humble servant etc. JAMES O'DONNELL

New York, 16th March, 1824

The Warden and Trustees of the
Parochial Church of our Lady of Montreal

Agreement
with
James O'Donnell

This Indenture

MADE THE FOURTH DAY OF MAY in the year of our Lord one thousand eight
hundred and twenty four between James O'Donnell of the City of New York
Architect, *of the First Part* and the Reverend Candide Michel Le Saulnier,
Acting Curate of the Parochial Church of our Lady of Montreal, Louis Guy,
Jean Philippe Leprohon, Francois Antoine La Rocque, Jean Bouthillier, Alexis
Laframboise, Julius Quesnel Esquires, and Messrs. Charles Simon Delorme
housebuilder, Pascal Persillier alias Lachapelle, Yeoman, Paschal Comte,
Pierre Pomminville and Joseph Chevallier, housebuilders, all of the Parish of
Montreal in the County and district of Montreal and province of Lower
Canada, forming the Majority of the Committee appointed to cause to be
erected the New Parochial Church of our Lady of Montreal in the City of
Montreal, in the said parish of Montreal, *of the Second Part*

Witnesseth — That the said party of the First part for and in consideration of the Covenants and Agreements hereinafter specified and set forth on the part and behalf of the said parties of the Second part to be done and performed, *Doth* hereby covenant promise and agree to and with the said parties of the Second part and their successors that he will furnish and provide all necessary working drawings for Masons, Stone cutters, Blacksmiths and Carpenters work for the New Parochial Church of our Lady of Montreal about to be erected in the said City of Montreal and will faithfully and truly conduct direct and superintend as Architect all and every part of the building of the said church agreeably and conformably thereto and to the approved plans of the said church already drawn by the said party of the First part and delivered to and remaining in the hands of the said parties of the Second part, signed "ne varietur" and to attend personally to the Execution of every part of the said Church according to said drawings and plans, and to give to the Master Mason, Master-Carpenter, Master-Stone Cutter and Master Blacksmith all necessary orders directions and explanations which shall be requisite to execute the whole and every part of the building of the said Church without any exception under the direction of three of the building Committee of the said Church; it being however fully understood that the said Master-Workmen and no others are to receive their instructions and directions from the said party of the First part so that they may be enabled to give orders and directions to their workmen to perfect the work. It being also understood that the said three persons of the said building Committee are to conduct the whole business with the said party of the First part and report to or communicate with the residue of said Committee so that the proceedings of the said party of the First part may be approved or disapproved of in due season.

And the said party of the First part doth hereby further covenant promise and agree to and with the said parties of the Second part that he will continue in their employ performing the duties and services aforesaid for the term of four years to be computed from the day of his departure from the City of New York which shall not be delayed beyond the Twelfth instant and will also serve them if they require it for such additional time after the expiration of said four years as may be necessary to complete the erecting and finishing of said church at the same rate of salary. And he hereby binds himself to see the whole Edifice done performed and executed with the greatest possible degree of accuracy, economy, solidity and beauty provided always that proper materials and workmen are furnished by the said parties of the Second part; it being hereby well understood and agreed by and between the said parties that the said party of the First part shall discharge personally all and singular the duties incumbent on his profession and capacity as an architect touching and regarding the whole and every part of said church; it being however also understood that he is to have nothing to do with keeping accounts of the time of workmen, clerkship, or with any of the money affairs of said Edifice.

And the said parties of the Second part for and in consideration of the due performance of the above covenants and agreements on the part of the said party of the First part *Do* covenant promise and agree to and with the said party of the First part for and in behalf of the Wardens and Trustees of the said Parochial Church of our Lady of Montreal that they will at all times during the continuance of this contract provide and furnish unto the said party of the First part an office for the convenient carrying on of his said business and all necessary paper quills, pencils ink and other needful articles of stationery for the making designing drawing and writing plans drawings orders directions and other things connected with or relating to the performance or execution of any part of the above mentioned church, and shall pay defray and reimburse unto the said party of the First part all travelling expenses to be by him incurred in going to the said City of Montreal on said service, so that immediately from and after his arrival at Montreal the said party of the First part shall pay and discharge all his own expenses, And they do further covenant and agree to pay unto him the said party of the First part the sum of Fifteen hundred Dollars current money of the State of New York for each and every year that he shall be so employed by them in the premises, the said sum to be paid in monthly payments at the end of each and every month deducting as is hereinafter provided — the first of which payments shall be made in one month after the day of the date of the departure of the party of the First part from the City of New York for Montreal aforesaid.

And it is hereby mutually understood and agreed that it shall and may be lawful for the said party of the First part to spend and devote to and for his own profit use and benefit all such time as he may spare during his service aforesaid without his above mentioned salary being on that account subjected to or liable to any reduction or diminution provided that he shall not neglect but on the contrary shall faithfully and diligently attend to the above work and discharge his duties above mentioned according to the true intent and meaning of these Presents.

And by way of security for the true and faithful performance of these Presents the said party of the First part *Doth* hereby agree that yearly and every year during the continuance of this agreement the said parties of the Second part may detain in their hands Five hundred Dollars of such his yearly salary, monthly proportional deductions to be for that part and to be paid over to the said party of the First part upon the due and faithful performance by him of his covenant in the premises. And further for the due performance of these Covenants the party of the First part *Doth* bind himself to the parties

Contract between the
Wardens and
O'Donnell

of the Second part in the sum of Two thousand Dollars as liquidated damages — IN WITNESS whereof the said parties have hereunto set their hands and seals at New York the fourth day of May One thousand eight hundred and twenty-four.

(Signed, Sealed & Delivered
in the presence of . . .
John Viale
Andrew Willcocks)

James O'Donnell

Candide Michel Le Saulnier
by his attorney Lewis Willcocks

Louis Guy
by his attorney Lewis Willcocks

Jean Philippe Leprohon
by his attorney Lewis Willcocks

Francois Antoine La Rocque
by his attorney Lewis Willcocks

Jean Bouthillier
by his attorney Lewis Willcocks

Alexis Laframboise
by his attorney Lewis Willcocks

Julius Quesnel
by his attorney Lewis Willcocks

Charles Simon Delorme
by his attorney Lewis Willcocks

Pascal Persillier alias Lachapelle
by his attorney Lewis Willcocks

Paschal Comte
by his attorney Lewis Willcocks

Pierre Pomminville
by his attorney Lewis Willcocks

Joseph Chevallier
by his attorney Lewis Willcocks

Notre-Dame houses a significant collection of Canadian painting and sculpture. Some of its more valuable works of art are housed in the Musée de Notre-Dame.[1] Those which are listed below are numbered according to the plan of the ground floor (*Plate* 12). Of the European paintings in Notre-Dame, the most important are six large canvases which were all in place in the old church by 1750.[2] Hung on the outer wall of the sanctuary, diagonally opposite altar 1 are copies of two seventeenth-century Italian paintings, "The Adoration of the Shepherds" and "The Presentation in the Temple." Opposite altar 2 are copies of "St. Ignatius of Loyola at Manrese" by Mignard, and an anonymous "Presentation of the Virgin in the Temple." The remaining two paintings also appear to be originals or copies of the seventeenth century: "The Nativity" and "The Holy Family," both in the sacristy. Also at the east end of the church are four paintings which were produced in Canada in the early nineteenth century. On the ceiling of the inner sacristy is a large tondo of the "Assumption of the Virgin" which was set into the middle of the ceiling of old Notre-Dame about 1810. It is a copy of a rectangular work by Charles Lebrun now hanging in the museum at Cherbourg, France. The copyist was Wilhelm von Moll Berczy, a German painter with English and Italian training who was then resident in Canada. Berczy also copied Lebrun's "Pentecost" (now in the Louvre), which has been placed over the altar of the Chapelle du Sacré-Coeur. In the corridor between the church and the chapel are two works by native Canadians, "St. Francis of Assisi" by Louis Dulongpré and an anonymous "St. Roch" which shows the present church of Notre-Dame in the background.

Between the windows and the doors of Notre-Dame there are fourteen ample wall areas which could have provided a splendid setting for paintings of the Stations of the Cross. In 1837 the Superior Quiblier commissioned such a cycle from Canada's leading painter, Antoine Plamondon (1804-1895), who had just returned from his studies in Paris under a pupil of Jacques-Louis David. In two years Plamondon produced fourteen very large and striking paintings in the heroic style of David. The wardens were forced to accept them, although they found their boldness displeasing. After 1847 the paintings left the church. Six now hang in the Musée des Beaux-Arts in Montreal, four in the parish church of Neuville, Quebec, and four apparently are lost.[3] The wardens then proceeded to buy three more sets of the Stations of the Cross, all of which seem to have been progressively worse. The first set (1839), by a M. Bowman of Quebec, Plamondon called disgusting.[4] The second (1847) was an ensemble created by twelve painters at the Accademia di San Luca in Rome. *Le Journal de Québec* called these works abominable and an insult to the artists practising in Quebec.[5] They are now in the church of Saint-Henri, Montreal. The third and final set came from France in 1876 and appears to copy older engravings.

In 1876 the original decoration of the columns and ceiling by Angelo Pienovi was replaced by the work of a M. Cleff from France. This decorative scheme is still retained but the ceiling, walls, and columns have been repainted and new twenty-two-carat gold leaf added at various intervals, most recently under M. Jean-Luc Perron in 1963. A number of copies or nineteenth century originals were at that time placed in the nave: "The Sacred Heart" in chapel 1; a copy of the "Madonna of the Rosary" by Sassoferrato and a tabernacle door in the style of Fra Angelico in chapel 2; "St. Ann" by Carnevali in chapel 3; "The Souls in Purgatory" by Pietro Minoccheri in chapel 4; paintings of "St. Joseph" and "St. Amable" in chapels 5 and 6; and finally a copy in the baptistry of the "Baptism of Christ" by Carlo Maratta in Santa Maria degli Angeli in Rome. The second gallery contains fourteen frescoes of the "Life of the Virgin" by L. G. Capello, an Italian who taught in Montreal in the 1870's.

The most interesting decorative programs in Notre-Dame were initiated by curés in 1891 and 1926. As the Chapelle du Sacré-Coeur neared completion in 1891, Curé Leon-Alfred Sentenne paid five young artists to study in Europe for three years on the condition that they later fill the blind clerestory of the chapel with their paintings. The five artists were Charles Gill, Joseph Saint-Charles, Henri Beau, J.-C. Franchère, and Ludger Larose. They studied at the Ecole des Beaux-Arts or at the Académie Julian in Paris and came under the influence of Puvis de Chavannes. They produced twelve original paintings: ten of them from the Bible and two from Canadian history. The latter were "The First Mass in Ville-Marie" and "The Oath of Dollard and his Companions," both by Saint-Charles.[6] Over the entrance were placed a copy of Léon Bonnet's "Christ on the Cross" and a huge copy of Raphael's "Disputà" by Ludger Larose.[7] The second commission was given by the late Mgr. Maurault in 1926 to Ozias Leduc to decorate the vault, windows, and over-door of the baptistry in a charming style which approximates Art Nouveau.[8]

The sculpture in Notre-Dame is more representative of French-Canadian art than the paintings. The oldest piece is an enormous wooden crucifix, nine feet high, which was carved for the old church in 1738 by Antoine Jourdain *dit* Labrosse.[9] Two other pieces from old Notre-Dame are the former high altar and a fragment from the baldachin which surmounted it. Both were made around 1812 by pupils in the school of Louis-Amable Quevillon (1749-1823) at Saint-Vincent-de-Paul, near Montreal.[10] The altar now serves in the chapel of St. Amable (6) (*Plate* 12) and exemplifies the provincial Rococo idiom of the school in its gilded tendrils, garlands, and swags.[11] The crown of the old baldachin is now in the church museum.

The pulpit, retable, and gallery railings that Paul Rollin and his assistants carved for O'Donnell in 1829 have all been replaced. The statues in the reredos and the reliefs immediately above the high altar are the work of Henri Bouriché and his assistant Chesneau.[12] Bouriché was also responsible for two more sensitive works, the "Presentation of the Virgin in the Temple" and a "Pietà," reliefs which have been installed in altars 2 and 4. Victor Bourgeau designed the reredos, choir stalls, and pulpit and entrusted their execution to the atelier of Georges Ducharme, just down the street from Notre-Dame.[13] The large white pine statues on the pulpit and those of "Daniel" and "Isaiah" flanking the high altar were made by Louis-Philippe Hébert *c.* 1884. The small statues on the pulpit and the models for the six plaster statues over the choir stalls appear to be the work of an associate of Ducharme named Dauphin. Ducharme supervised the erection of all the side altars and their canopies except altar 6, which was older, and altars 7 and 8, which are of more recent date. The three wooden entrance vestibules were constructed in the Gothic style around 1955.

Under Perrault and Mesnard, successors to Victor Bourgeau, the nave received new pews and confessionals around 1888 and two special pews, the *banc d'oeuvre* and *banc des juges*, opposite the pulpit. These are remarkable for their ornate relief-work. The same architects built the sacristy and the Chapelle du Sacré-Coeur and employed a large number of craftsmen to carve almost every available surface on the walls and ceiling. Arthur Vincent designed the overall decoration and carved the high altar and the reredos of the chapel. Two powerful sculptural groups, "Ecce Homo" and "The Kiss of Judas," were carved in oak in 1892 by L.-O. Gratton of Montreal and placed before the west wall of the chapel. They are among the finest and least academic works of sculpture in the church. From the twentieth century there are at least four wood statues in Notre-Dame: "St. Therese of Lisieux" and a

"Holy Family" by Elzéar Soucy and the recent portraits of the Venerable Mère d'Youville and the Venerable Marguerite Bourgeois by Sylvia Daoust.

In 1929 Notre-Dame received its most significant works of art of this century. The then Curé Maurault commissioned Jean-Baptiste Legacé, professor of art at l'Université de Montréal, to design eleven stained glass windows for the side aisles. Maurault selected eleven scenes from the history of Montreal which were then illustrated by Legacé and executed in glass by the atelier of Chigot in Limoges (*Plate* 50).[14] These windows provide a concise history of the city from the arrival of Jacques Cartier in 1535 to the consecration of Notre-Dame in 1929. They delight the eye with their bold colours and striking compositions. Of the many additions to Notre-Dame since its construction, these eleven windows accord most fully with the style and conceptions of both O'Donnell and Bourgeau.

𝔈NTRIES MARKED * are reproduced here. Entries marked † are reproduced in Charles de Volpi and P. S. Winkworth, *Montréal: Recueil Iconographique — A Pictorial Record* (Montreal, 1963), 2 vols.

1. One hundred and seventy-three drawings in pencil, pen and ink, and wash by James O'Donnell for Notre-Dame, 1824-1829. Archives of Notre-Dame. (Ten plans and sketches *)

2. Water-colour of Notre-Dame by John Drake, 1826. Archives du Séminaire de Québec. Based on a lost elevation by O'Donnell.

3. Montreal from Mount Royal, showing Notre-Dame under construction. Lithograph by T. M. Baynes after Lieutenant Hornbrook, probably 1827. (†)

4. Two drawings of the interior and one of the exterior of Notre-Dame by John O'Kill, 1829. Archives du Séminaire de Québec. (*) The third drawing was engraved in 1829 and printed in New York, probably by James Smillie. (†)

5. Old and new Notre-Dame churches seen from Place Jacques-Cartier (†) and from Place d'Armes. (*†) Two engravings by Robert A. Sproule, 1830.

6. Exterior of Notre-Dame, lithograph by John Wells, New York, 1834. (*†)

7. The interior and exterior of Notre-Dame, the church seen from Mount Royal and from the St. Lawrence; four steel engravings by W. H. Bartlett, *c.* 1838. Published by N. P. Willis, *Canadian Scenery* (London, 1842). (One and two *; all †)

8. Notre-Dame seen from the suburbs of Montreal, a pencil sketch by J. B. B. Estcourt, 1838. Public Archives of Canada. (*)

9. Notre-Dame seen from the St. Lawrence, water-colour by Blainfield (?), 1842. Formerly Reford Collection, Montreal. (*)

10. Two views of the first and second great bells of Notre-Dame. Printed by A. R. Grieve and Thomas Turner, London, 1843 and 1847. (Both †)

11. Notre-Dame from Place d'Armes, engraved by John Murray, c. 1850. (†)

12. Photograph of the exterior by William Notman, c. 1860. Canadian Historic Sites Division, Department of Indian Affairs and Northern Development, Ottawa.

13. Photograph of the interior by William Notman, 1860. Notman Photographic Archives, McCord Museum, McGill University, Montreal. (*)

14. Four lithographs of the interior of Notre-Dame in *L'Opinion Publique*: "Return of the Papal Zouaves," March 1870; "The Distribution of Ashes on Ash Wednesday," March 9, 1871; James Weston, "The Funeral of Sir Georges-Etienne Cartier," June 26, 1873; and Eugène Haberer, "Mass of the Société Saint-Jean-Baptiste," July 2, 1874. (Second and third*)

15. Photograph of the interior by J. G. Parks, c. 1880. Canadian Historic Sites Division, Department of Indian Affairs and Northern Development, Ottawa.

Notes to II: NOTRE-DAME AND SAINT-SULPICE

1. On the history of this association, see Marie-Claire Daveluy, *La Société de Notre-Dame de Montréal 1639-1663* (Montreal, 1965).

2. Louis-Adolphe Huguet-Latour, *Annuaire de Ville-Marie*, part I, pp. 344-45, and *Le Monde*, October 31, 1885, p. 6.

3. *Le Troisième Centenaire de Saint-Sulpice*, p. 67.

4. William Benett Munro, *The Seigniorial System in Canada* (New York, 1907), pp. 10-15 and 85-100.

5. François Dollier de Casson, *A History of Montreal: 1640-1672*, p. 28.

6. André-Marie-J.-J. Dupin, *Opinion of Mr. Dupin, Advocate, of the Royal Court of Paris, on the Rights of the Seminary of Montreal, in Canada*, p. 1.

7. *Considérations sur les biens du Séminaire de Montréal* (Montreal, n.d. [1824?]), p. 6. See also Georges-E. Baillargeon, *La Survivance du régime seigneurial à Montréal* (Montreal, 1968).

8. Olivier Maurault, *Saint-Jacques de Montréal*, pp. 10-11.

9. Olivier Maurault, *La Paroisse: Histoire de l'Eglise Notre-Dame de Montréal*, 2d. ed. rev., 1957, pp. 177-74.

10. Étienne-Michel Faillon, *Histoire de la Colonie Française en Canada*, III, p. 379.

11. Olivier Maurault, "Dollier de Casson," *Revue Trimestrielle Canadienne*, IV, p. 368.

12. Faillon, *Histoire de la Colonie Française*, p. 380.

13. Maurault, "Dollier de Casson," pp. 366-68.

14. Faillon, *Histoire de la Colonie Française*, pp. 380-81. Alan Gowans, in *Church Architecture in New France*, pp. 64 and 112, cites a document of 1683 which describes Notre-Dame as 129 feet long and 38 feet wide.

15. The third church is described at length in Maurault, *La Paroisse*, pp. 13-25.

16. Henri Gauthier, *Sulpitiana*, p. 239.

17. Joseph Bouchette, *The British Dominions in North America*, p. 215.

18. Maurault, *La Paroisse*, pp. 18 and 27.

19. Isaac Weld, *Travels through the States of North America and the Provinces of Upper and Lower Canada, During the Years 1795, 1796 and 1797* (London, 1799), p. 178.

20. Huguet-Latour, *Annuaire de Ville-Marie*, p. 379, and Maurault, *La Paroisse*, p. 21.

21. Letter from Mrs. Sarah Charland to the wardens of Notre-Dame, April 14, 1824, requesting payment for the plan of a new church drawn by Louis Charland in 1819. (Unless otherwise noted, all manuscripts cited are preserved in the archives of the church of Notre-Dame.)

Notes to II:
Notre-Dame and
Saint-Sulpice

22. *Le Troisième Centenaire de Saint-Sulpice*, p. 79.

23. Gowans, *Church Architecture in New France*, p. 138.

24. Huguet-Latour, *Annuaire de Ville-Marie*, p. 350.

25. J.-B.-A. Ferland, *Biographical Notice of Joseph-Octave Plessis, Bishop of Quebec*, pp. 97-102.

26. *Ibid.*, p. 106.

27. *Ibid.*, p. 114.

28. *Ibid.*, p. 141.

29. *Ibid.*

30. *Ibid.*, p. 151.

31. *Ibid.*, p. 156.

32. "On m'a envoyé un long mémoire pour prouver par raison démonstrative que tous les honneurs que je vous abandonne et auxquels vous prétendez sont abusifs. Je ne disputerai point avec l'auteur; mais je ferai passer en cour de Rome mon mandement du vingt février et me soumettrai au jugement du saint-siège. En attendant, ne contestez pas; mettez les procédés de votre côté. Si on vous pousse, reculez-vous. A défaut du trône, contentez-vous d'un prie-dieu; à défaut d'un prie-dieu, mettez-vous sur le bout d'un banc, ou ce qui serait encore mieux, cessez d'assister à la paroisse qui n'est plus cathédrale que toute autre église de la ville; et adoptez l'église de l'Hôtel-Dieu ou toute autre." (J.-B.-A. Ferland, *Mgr. Joseph-Octave Plessis, Evêque de Québec*, p. 243.)

33. Letter from Mr. Gradwell in Rome to Plessis, January 19, 1824, in "Inventaire de la correspondence de Mgr. Joseph-Octave Plessis, 1816 à 1825," *Rapport de l'Archiviste de la Province de Québec pour 1928-29*, p. 181.

34. *Ibid.*, p. 207. Letter from Plessis to Bishop Poynter of London, November 12, 1825.

35. Louis Guy and Jacques Viger, "Dénombrement du Comté de Montréal fait en 1825 par Louis Guy et Jacques Viger," microfilm copy in the Bibliothèque de la Ville de Montréal.

36. Maurault, *La Paroisse*, p. 44.

37. "Dieu, qui sait tirer sa gloire de tout, Nos très chers frères, a pris occasion des contrariétés par lesquelles Mgr. l'Evêque de Telmesse a été éprouvé depuis le commencement de son Episcopat, pour procurer à votre ville une église de plus, dont la magnifique structure s'est élevée comme par enchantement et est parvenue à sa fin avec une rapidité dont les étrangers et les indigènes sont également surpris." (Pastoral letter from Plessis to the Catholics of Montreal, September 12, 1825, quoted in Léon Pouliot, "Il y a cent ans: le démembrement de la paroisse Notre-Dame," *Revue d'Histoire de l'Amérique Française*, XIX [1965], p. 355.)

Notes to III: REBUILDING NOTRE-DAME

1. "Rapport du Comité . . . pour aviser aux moyens qu'il seroient convenable d'adopter pour remedier aux inconvéniens qui résultent de la petitisse de l'Eglise Paroissiale," September 2, 1822.

2. See Léon Pouliot, "Il y a cent ans: le démembrement de la paroisse Notre-Dame," *Revue d'Histoire de l'Amérique Française*, XIX (1965), pp. 350-83.

3. "Mais un tel accroissement de la population Catholique de la paroisse n'est pas du tout probable. Votre Comité croit qu'à l'exception des Grandes Solemnités il n'y a guère que le quart des paroissiens qui doivent ou qui peuvent assister ensemble à la Grande Messe paroissiale, d'où il conclut qu'une Eglise qui contiendrait huit à neuf mille personnes suffirait largement au besoin de la paroisse pour cinquante ou soixante ans à venir *pour le moins*.

"Il a été calculé qu'une Eglise qui aurait cent vingt pieds de large en dedans et deux cents pieds de long dans la nef, non compris le choeur, et ayant deux rangées de galeries pourrait asseoir ce nombre de personnes en même temps que la voix du prédicateur pourrait se faire bien entendre de toutes parts." ("Rapport du Comité. . . .")

4. "Rapport du Comité. . . ."

5. François-Antoine LaRocque, "The Missouri Journal 1804-1805," in L.-R. Masson, *Les Bourgeois de la Compagnie de Nord-Ouest* (Quebec, 1889), I, pp. 299-313, and *Journal of Larocque from the Assiniboine to the Yellowstone, 1805*, ed. L. J. Burpee (Ottawa, 1910).

6. This and the following information is derived from a number of sources, principally Hector Berthelot, *Montréal: Le Bon Vieux Temps*, and E.-Z. Massicotte, *Faits curieux de l'histoire du Canada* (Montreal, 1922).

7. Merrill Denison in his *History of the Bank of Montreal*, I, p. 76, notes that 47 per cent of the bank's original shareholders in 1817 lived in New York and Boston. By far the best book on this period in French Canada is Fernand Ouellet's *Histoire Economique et Sociale du Québec 1760-1850*.

8. Romuald Trudeau, "Mes Tablettes," October 7, 1822, Bibliothèque Nationale, Montreal.

9. Letter from Plessis to LaRocque, February 7, 1823, in *Rapport de l'Archiviste de la Province de Québec pour 1928-29*, p. 166.

10. *Ibid.*, pp. 174 and 176. Letters from Plessis to Curé Alexis Leclerc, September 24 and October 17, 1823.

11. Trudeau, "Mes Tablettes," June 19, 1823.

12. *Ibid.*, June 15, 1823.

Notes to III:
Rebuilding
Notre-Dame

13. "de faire venir des Etats-Unis ou d'Europe un architecte, s'il le juge convenable." (Minutes of the building committee, August 24, 1823.)

14. Letter from Thavenet to the building committee, October 28, 1823.

15. On the cathedral of Saint-Jacques see Alan Gowans, "Notre-Dame de Montréal," *Journal of the Society of Architectural Historians*, XI (March 1952), pp. 21-23, and Olivier Maurault, *Saint-Jacques de Montréal*.

16. Jacques Viger, "Ma Sabredache," VII, p. 171. Archives du Séminaire de Québec, Quebec.

17. According to a letter from Bouthillier to O'Donnell, September 18, 1823, and a second recommendation from Willcocks to the building committee, April 28, 1824. In 1824 O'Donnell lived at 55 Water Street, New York, and Willcocks at Number 18.

18. "M. Bouthillier a fait rapport que arrivant à New-York il avait fait connaissance avec un architecte que l'on disait être très habile, et qu'on le lui avait fortement recommandé comme une personne très capable de fournir les plans nécessaires pour la construction de notre nouvelle Eglise, et que cet architecte était connu ici par M. Vanderlyn, de qui on pouvait avoir de nouveau renseignements à son sujet.

"Messrs. LaRocque et Quesnel sont chargés en conséquence de voir M. Vanderlyn et de prendre de lui des informations sur la capacité et les talents de M. O'Donnell, l'architecte en question." (Minutes of the building committee, September 12, 1823.)

19. Letter to the author from Mrs. C. L. Arnold, Superintendent of the Senate House Museum, Vanderlyn Archives, Kingston, New York, 1965.

Notes to IV: JAMES O'DONNELL

1. Information from the Convert Rolls in the Four Courts, Dublin, courtesy of Mrs. Eilish Ellis, and from the will of O'Donnell, November 14, 1829, Archives Judiciaires, Palais de Justice, Montreal, located with the aid of the director of the archives, M. Jean-Jacques Lefebvre.

2. See Desmond Guinness, *Portrait of Dublin*, and Maurice Craig, *Dublin 1660-1860*.

3. John Summerson, *Architecture in Britain 1530-1830*, pp. 227-28.

4. The drawing is reproduced courtesy of the National Library of Ireland. It was the gift of the Pakenham-Mahon family of Stokestown, Co. Roscommon, for whom it may have been planned.

5. See Patrick Henchy, "Francis Johnston, Architect, 1760-1829," *Dublin Historical Review*, XI, no. 1 (1949-1950), pp. 1-16.

6. See Guinness, *Portrait of Dublin*, for illustrations of Johnston's St. George's Church and Maurice Craig and the Knight of Glin, *Irish Architectural Drawings* (Dublin, 1965), for illustrations of Johnston's General Post Office, Royal Hibernian Academy, and a "Gothick Pulpit."

7. Henchy, "Francis Johnston," p. 5.

8. See Marcus Whiffen, "The Progeny of St. Martin in the Fields," *Architectural Review*, C (July 1946), p. 5.

9. Craig and the Knight of Glin, *Irish Architectural Drawings*, p. 5.

10. This was the type of training that Wyatt gave his assistants. See Frank Beckwith, *Thomas Taylor, Regency Architect* (Leeds, 1949), p. 12.

11. These buildings will be illustrated and discussed in the author's forthcoming study on O'Donnell in the *Journal of the Society of Architectural Historians*.

12. The drawings are numbers 169-78 in the McComb Collection, The New-York Historical Society, New York.

13. Edmund Blunt, *The Picture of New York, or the Stranger's Guide to the Commercial Metropolis of the United States* (New York, 1828), p. 217.

14. "Records of Christ Church Corporation," Archives of Christ Church, New York. O'Donnell was paid $500 on April 16, 1822, an unspecified amount on May 7, 1822, $30 on August 20, 1822, $15 on May 5, 1823, and $50 on August 10, 1823. Information kindly supplied by Miss Betty Ezequelle, formerly Assistant Curator of Maps and Prints, The New-York Historical Society.

15. Mary Bartlett Cowdrey, *American Academy of Fine Arts and American Art-Union Exhibition Record 1816-1852* (New York, 1953), II, p. 273.

16. Adolf Placzek, "Design for Columbia College, 1813," *Journal of the Society of Architectural Historians*, XI (May 1952), pp. 22-23.

Notes to V: THE DESIGN OF NOTRE-DAME

1. Suggested in the letter from Bouthillier to O'Donnell, September 18, 1823.

2. Letter from O'Donnell to the building committee, March 16, 1824.

3. On the twin-towered church in France, see Henry-Russell Hitchcock, *Architecture: Nineteenth and Twentieth Centuries*, p. 45, n. 1.

4. Mention of models in wood in minutes of the building committee, July 29, 1825.

5. Minutes of the building committee, August 7, 1829. The most important plans were stolen by two Americans, *c.* 1840. "Assemblée Annuelle de la Société d'Archéologie," *Le Canada*, Montreal, XV, December 22, 1917, p. 10.

6. Letter from O'Donnell to the building committee, January 14, 1824.

7. Marcus Whiffen, *Stuart and Georgian Churches*, p. 80.

8. See the plans in M. H. Port, *Six Hundred New Churches*.

9. A popular example was W. F. Pocock's *Designs for Churches and Chapels* (London, 1824), in which the great majority of Gothic plans are rectangular.

10. "ce monsieur dit que les plans de notre église sont généralement approuvés, et que déjà l'on bâtit une église sur le même plan à New-York, mais sur de plus petits dimensions." (Minutes of the building committee, April 20, 1824.)

11. "The Churches of New York," *Putnam's Monthly*, II (1853), p. 237.

12. These details are taken from a plan of the church after mid-century alterations, in the Geneology and Local History Room of the New York Public Library; from John Coolidge, "Gothic Revival Churches in New England and New York," pp. 54-59, and from George E. de Mille, *St. Thomas Church in the City and County of New York 1823-1954*.

13. Anthony Garvan, "The Protestant Plain Style before 1630," *Journal of the Society of Architectural Historians*, IX (October 1950), pp. 6 and 7.

14. "The Churches of New York," p. 237.

15. John Henry Hopkins, *Essay on Gothic Architecture*, plate 6, figure 13.

16. The archives of Notre-Dame contain a plan of the sanctuary of the old church as it appeared in 1819, by Abbé Bédard.

17. See Jacques-François Blondel, *Architecture Française*, II, plate 167.

18. Alfred Sandham, *Montreal and Its Fortifications*, p. 10.

19. *Ibid.*, pp. 11-22.

20. Letter to the author from H. M. Colvin, Fellow of St. John's College, Oxford, 1965.

21. Margery A. Hall, "History of St. Paul's Church, Fairfax Parish, Alexandria, Virginia," p. 3. On Latrobe (1764-1820), see Talbot Hamlin, *Benjamin Henry Latrobe* (New York, 1955).

22. Letter from Latrobe to the Reverend Mr. Wilmer, July 14, 1817. Copy in the Maryland Historical Society, Baltimore.

23. O'Donnell's name is not mentioned, so far as the author could discover, in any of Latrobe's correspondence in the Library of Congress or in the Maryland Historical Society.

24. Letter from O'Donnell to the building committee, December 8, 1823.

25. For a full analysis of the twin-towered church in the early American Gothic Revival, see Coolidge, "Gothic Revival Churches in New England and New York," pp. 51-63.

26. Alan Gowans, *Church Architecture in New France*, pp. 76-80, and letter to the author, 1965.

27. There was an engraving and description of the synagogue in the *New York Mirror*, VII, September 26, 1829, reproduced in Oliver Larkin's *Art and Life in America* (New York, 1966), p. 155. Information kindly supplied by Miss Betty Ezequelle.

28. According to a water colour made from an elevation in 1826 by John Drake, "Album de Jacques Viger," plate XXI, Archives du Séminaire de Québec.

29. All exterior dimensions are taken from the measured drawings made in 1931 by Eugène Saint-Jean, architect.

30. Interview with M. Pierre-S. Beaudry, president of B.G.L. Ingénieurs Associés, Montreal, 1968.

31. Hopkins, *Essay on Gothic Architecture*, pp. 45-46.

32. *The Centenary of the Bank of Montreal 1817-1917* (Montreal, 1917), p. 39.

Notes to VI: CONSTRUCTION AND DECORATION

1. This and other tenders for Notre-Dame were parodied two weeks later in *The Scribbler*, a Montreal humour weekly:

Tenders Wanted

Sealed tenders will be received from the 1st of July next, till it is convenient to stop; at the subscribers' office, opposite No. 10, St. Tantony's Suburb for the supplying of a few thousand quarters, halves, or wholes, of the first rate lean mutton, for the use of the St. Tantony soup and chop-house and lanthom-manufactory. Persons desirous of contracting for the same, will state the price per four quarters. Tenders to be endorsed "*Tenders for furnishing mutton*"; and will be received till twelve o'clock at night, every day, by the subscribers, who are appointed agents for the above.

Fryingpan & Co.

N.B. *Gentlemen* will knock at the back gate; but *blackguards* will come to the front-door. (*The Scribbler*, Montreal, June 24, 1824, p. 221.)

The satire seems to be directed not at the *Fabrique* but at one of the "blackguards," the stone supplier John Redpath, whom *The Scribbler*, on May 13, 1824, had accused of cheating his stonecutters of their pay.

2. Harold Poitras, "Notre Dame Renovations," *Montreal Star*, July 12, 1962.

3. "Memorandum of Timber wanted for the use of the new Catholic Parish Church now building in Montreal, *viz.* Montreal, 11th October 1824." Collection Baby, Bibliothèque de l'Université de Montréal.

4. Interview with M. Pierre-S. Beaudry, 1968.

5. Thomas Ritchie, *Canada Builds: 1867-1967*, p. 181.

6. Letter from O'Donnell to the building committee, April 3, 1827.

7. "Nous dirons, à propos de la pose de la première pierre de l'édifice, que la cérémonie avait attiré un immense concours de spectateurs et de curieux. L'enthousiasme fut si grand, qu'après un discours où M. O'Donnell expliquait ses plans et la physionomie de l'église nouvelle, la foule, transportée, força le brave homme à s'asseoir sur l'énorme bloc qu'on allait sceller avec l'appareil d'usage.

"Alors, à l'aide de cabestans, que manoeuvraient de vigoureux gaillards, l'on éleva dans l'air architecte et granit, et là, tandis que tous deux tournaient lentement dans l'espace, la masse enfiévrée, délirante, battit des mains, poussa des hourrahs, des bravos, des vivats, à faire rompre les cables. Ceux-ci tinrent bon heureusement, et, pendant dix minutes au moins, M. O'Donnell fut l'objet d'une ovation comme jamais son collègue défunt, Michel Ange, n'en avait obtenu de son vivant." (*Le National*, Montreal, March 18, 1876.)

There are contemporary accounts in the *Montreal Gazette and Commercial Advertiser*, September 4, 1824, and *Le Spectateur Canadien*, Montreal, September 4, 1824.

8. Minutes of the building committee, April 15, 1825.

9. Minutes of the building committee, October 20, 1824.

10. Ritchie, *Canada Builds: 1867-1967*, p. 67.

11. "Description et désignation des Bienfonds de la Fabrique de Montréal," October 14, 1826. Archives de la Chancellerie de l'Archevêché de Montréal, file 901.140.

12. Hector Berthelot, *Montréal: Le Bon Vieux Temps*, I, p. 113.

13. Alain Forêt, "L'Eglise Notre-Dame 'prend les forces'," *Le Petit Journal*, Montreal, September 2, 1962.

14. Letter from Cox to the building committee, December 21, 1827.

15. Minutes of the building committee, May 22, 1828.

16. Milner's niche appeared as figure 33 on plate VII of his *Treatise on the Ecclesiastical Architecture of England*.

17. John Henry Hopkins, *Essay on Gothic Architecture*, p. vi.

18. Robert L. Alexander, "Architecture and Aristocracy: The Cosmopolitan Style of Latrobe and Godefroy," *Maryland Historical Magazine*, LVI (1961), p. 233.

19. Letter from Latrobe to Robert Mills, February 13, 1808. Copy in the Maryland Historical Society.

20. Letter from Latrobe to Christian Latrobe in London, February 6, 1805. Copy in the Maryland Historical Society.

21. Lecture by Ovide Lapalice, "Les Bancs de Notre-Dame depuis 1642," reported in *La Presse*, Montreal, December 14, 1932.

22. Olivier Maurault, *La Paroisse: Histoire de l'Eglise Notre-Dame de Montréal*, p. 228.

23. *La Minerve*, Montreal, July 9, 1829, and July 16, 1829; *The Irish Vindicator*, Montreal, July 17, 1829.

24. "Compte rendue du Comité de Bâtisse de l'Eglise Paroissiale à la Fabrique de Montréal," September 1, 1832. Archives de la Chancellerie de l'Archevêché de Montréal, file 901.140.

25. "M. LaRocque a ensuite demandé pour lui et les autres membres du Comité de Bâtisse que le dit Comité soit maintenant déchargé. Sur quoi il a été RÉSOLU que cette Fabrique est parfaitement satisfaite de l'oeuvre du dit Comité de Bâtisse. Remercier tous ses membres, tant ceux qui sont Marguilliers que ceux qui ne le sont pas du zèle, du soin et de l'activité qu'ils ont mis à faire bâtir la nouvelle église. Et ratifiant tout ce qu'en cette qualité et à cette fin, ils ont fait leur donner une pleine et entière décharge." (Minutes of the wardens' meeting, September 16, 1832.)

Notes to VI: Construction and Decoration

Notes to VII: CRITICAL APPRAISAL

1. Pierre-Louis Morin, "Description de l'Eglise Paroissiale de la Ville de Montréal ou Ville-Marie," *Mélanges Religieux*, II, pp. 354-56.

2. *Le National*, IV, March 18, 1876; and Douglas Borthwick, *Historical and Graphical Gazeteer of Montreal*, p. 112.

3. Letter from LaRocque to O'Donnell, March 15, 1824.

4. Letter from O'Donnell to the building committee, January 27, 1827.

5. Asher Benjamin, *The American Builder's Companion*, plates 56 and 57.

6. Receipt of Horatio Gates for payment of £25 from the wardens, 1825.

7. Minutes of the American Presbyterian Congregation, December 6, 1824, courtesy of the Reverend Mr. N. M. Slaughter of the Erskine and American United Church, Montreal.

8. Newton Bosworth, *Hochelaga depicta*, pp. 148-49 and engraved view.

9. Will 170 in the files of notary N.-B. Doucet, Archives Judiciaires, Palais de Justice, Montreal.

10. Merrill Denison, *History of the Bank of Montreal*, I, p. 191.

11. "M. Quiblier, pour vaincre les dernières répugnances d'O'Donnell, lui aurait offert d'être enterrer dans l'église — Ce qui aurait determiné la conversion aux images de l'émotion." (Pierre Rousseau, "Notes sur l'Eglise Notre-Dame.") Rousseau's account is given partial confirmation in the report of "S.N." and in the tomb epitaph. The grave site is number 202 (possibly indicated in O'Donnell's handwriting) in *Plate* 11.

12. S.N., *The Jesuit*, p. 203. The oath of conversion is in the "Régistre des Abjurations, Marriages, Réhabités et Baptêmes," November 14, 1829; the statement of burial is in the "Livre de Baptêmes, Marriages, et Sépulchres," February 1, 1830.

13.   Ci-Git
                    JAMES O'DONNELL, Ecuier
                    Architecte, Né en Irlande
                    et décédé en cette Ville
                    le 28 Janvier 1830
                    âgé de 56 ans.

Il travailla cinq ans à cette église dont il donna le plan et dirigea les travaux avec zèle et intelligence. Puis embrassa la foi Catholique et voulut que ses cendres reposassent en ce lieu. Son désintéressement, ses talents, et sa probité lui méritent l'estime de cette paroisse; et les Marguilliers ont consacré ce Monument à sa Mémoire.

Requiescat in pace

[Here Lies
JAMES O'DONNELL, Esq.
Architect, Born in Ireland
and died in this City
28 January 1830
aged 56.

For five years he worked on this church for which he made the plan and directed the works with industry and intelligence. He then embraced the Catholic faith and wished his remains to rest in this place. His disinterested nature, his talents, and his honesty earned him the esteem of this parish, and the Wardens have dedicated this Monument to his Memory.

Requiescat in pace]

14. James Silk Buckingham, *Canada, Nova Scotia, New Brunswick and the other British Provinces in North America, with a plan of National Colonization*, p. 111.

15. Thomas Storrow Brown, "Montreal in 1818," *New Dominion Monthly*, March 1870, p. 21.

16. "ces immenses constructions des tours, que l'on n'avait plus ôsé aborder depuis près de trois siècles dans le monde chrétien." (*La Minerve*, Montreal, April 27, 1866.)

17. Morin, in his "Description de l'Eglise Paroissiale de la Ville de Montréal," p. 355, said that Notre-Dame was second in size only to St. Peter's. John MacGregor, in *British America*, II, p. 506, called it superior to any Gothic church, save Paris, Amiens, and Rouen.

18. Eliot Warburton, *Hochelaga: or, England in the New World*, I, p. 114.

19. Marcus Whiffen, *Stuart and Georgian Churches*, p. 83.

20. B. W. A. Sleigh, *Pine Forests and Hacmatack Clearings, or Travel, Life and Adventure in the British North American Provinces*, pp. 237-38. Despite the odd title, Sleigh's impressions from his trip of 1846 are most interesting. The reference to an altar similar to that in St. Peter's must have been taken from a much earlier description. The allusion is to the Corinthian baldachin of old Notre-Dame which was placed in the new church (see *Plate* 14) until 1830. Sleigh was also wrong about the composition of the choir.

21. "D'aussi loin qu'on voit poindre de la ville de Montréal, on aperçoit les tours de notre magnifique église. On ne peut s'empêcher d'admirer, en approchant, ses proportions grandioses, son genre d'architecture simple, austère et solonnel comme la religion romaine. Mais combien est grand le désappointement en franchissant le seuil. Vous vous attendez à un intérieur de cathédrale sombre, grave, imposant comme l'idée de Dieu qui y réside. Au lieu de cela, c'est quelque chose de vague, de terne, de froid, d'inachevé; à la voûte une bigarrure, un barbouillage de couleurs bleues et grises sans poésie et sans goût, aux murs des taches sales et nombreuses, de longues fissures, des traces de pluie et d'humidité." ("Histoire de la Semaine," *La Revue Canadienne*, I, June 14, 1845.)

22. Joseph Bouchette, *The British Dominions in North America*, pp. 217-22.

23. "The Parish Church of Notre-Dame," *Montreal Herald and Daily Commercial Gazette*, March 2, 1875.

24. On the history of the bells of Notre-Dame, see Olivier Maurault, *La Paroisse: Histoire de l'Eglise Notre-Dame de Montréal*, pp. 133-54, and "Histoire de la Semaine," *La Revue Canadienne*, I, May 31, 1845.

25. *Le Journal de Québec*, Quebec, October 11, 1864.

26. In 1856, however, the Sulpicians also took over the administration of the church of Saint-Jacques.

27. J. E. Alexander, *Transatlantic Sketches*, II, p. 192.

28. For example, see E. T. Coke, *A Subaltern's Furlough*, pp. 334-35.

29. See especially Napoléon Bourassa, "Causerie Artistique," *La Revue Canadienne*, n.s., IV (1867), pp. 796-97, and his article in *La Minerve*, July 3, 1872.

30. Henry David Thoreau, *A Yankee in Canada, with Anti-Slavery and Reform Papers*, pp. 12-13.

Notes to VII:
Critical Appraisal

31. Edmund Burke, *A Philosophical Inquiry into the Origin of Our Ideas of the Sublime and Beautiful*, pp. 103-5. O'Donnell did in fact associate Gothic with the sublime in his letter to the building committee of March 16, 1824.

32. John Henry Hopkins, *Essay on Gothic Architecture*, p. 12.

33. William Dean Howells, *Their Wedding Journey*, p. 198.

34. "L'église Notre-Dame, pourvue de vastes galeries, elles-mêmes disposées en gradins, est sans doute le plus colossal *auditorium* que possède la chrétienté....Il se trouve, par surcroît, que ce gigantesque vaisseau est merveilleusement sonore, et que, sans fatigue, sans cri, on est entendu de partout. Et c'est une sensation délicieuse, que je ne pense pas qu'on puisse éprouver ailleurs, de causer à mi-voix, avec dix mille âmes." (Pierre Vignot, *Carême de Montréal*, pp. 6 and 8.)

Notes to VIII: VICTOR BOURGEAU AND NOTRE-DAME

1. Léon Pouliot, "Il y a cent ans: le démembrement de la paroisse Notre-Dame," *Revue d'Histoire de l'Amérique Française*, XIX (1965), p. 350.

2. Henri Gauthier, *Sulpitiana*, p. 242.

3. A number of these plans are reproduced in the first edition of Olivier Maurault, *La Paroisse: Histoire de l'Eglise Notre-Dame de Montréal.*

4. On Bourgeau see Alan Gowans, "The Baroque Revival in Québec," *Journal of the Society of Architectural Historians*, XIV, pp. 8-14; Gérard Morisset in *La Patrie*, Montreal, May 7, 1950; Olivier Maurault, *Saint-Jacques de Montréal*, pp. 53-55; and Mary Ann Coyle, "Victor Bourgeau, Architect: A Biographical Sketch," unpublished manuscript, 1960, School of Architecture, McGill University, Montreal.

5. Bills for various plans and models, 1855-58.

6. Minutes of the wardens, February 15, 1857.

7. Maurault, *La Paroisse* (1st ed., 1929), p. 111.

8. Minutes of the wardens, June 27, 1869.

9. *Le Franc Parleur*, Montreal, V, May 21, 1875.

10. Minutes of the wardens, July 3, 1876.

11. *Montreal Herald and Daily Commercial Gazette*, March 2, 1875.

12. Maurault, *La Paroisse*, p. 77, quoting Laroche, *Un Sculpteur Religieux* (Angers, 1907), p. 86.

13. Louis Réau, *Iconographie de l'Art Chrétien* (Paris, 1956), II, part 1, *passim*.

14. It is likely that these were enlargements of statues made of the same six saints by Monsieur Dauphin in 1864 to fill the small niches on the facade. [*Journal de Québec*, October 11, 1864.]

15. Letter from Lewis Willcocks to the building committee, April 30, 1828.

16. *Le National*, IV, March 18, 1876.

17. The design is in the archives of Notre-Dame. See also the memorial on Bourgeau in *La Minerve*, March 22, 1888.

18. On Hébert see Gilles Dostaler, "Philippe Hébert," *La Presse*, Montreal, December 14, 1963.

19. There is a rare view in Russell and Triggs, *Portrait of a Period: A Collection of Notman Photographs 1856-1915* (Montreal, 1967), plate 80.

20. Minutes of the wardens, June 29, 1898.

Notes to IX: NOTRE-DAME AS A FRENCH-CANADIAN CHURCH

1. "un véritable monument national, où le sentiment religieux et patriotique des Canadiens français s'est exprimé avec un éclat incomparable." (Olivier Maurault, *La Paroisse: Histoire de l'Eglise Notre-Dame de Montréal*, p. 215.)

2. "l'Irlandais protestant James O'Donnell, de New-York, . . . ignore tout de notre tradition et de notre climat. Et quel est ce style gothique que l'architecte impose arbitrairement à la nouvelle Notre-Dame? C'est un gothique troubadour d'origine anglaise, de formes sèches et coupantes, d'une mouluration mesquine et d'une construction irrationnelle." (Gérard Morisset, *L'Architecture en Nouvelle-France*, p. 87.)

3. Alan Gowans, "Notre-Dame de Montréal," *Journal of the Society of Architectural Historians*, XI (March 1952), p. 25.

4. Robert Hubbard, "Canadian Gothic," *Architectural Review*, CXVI (August 1954), p. 102. This opinion was given wider readership in Henry-Russell Hitchcock, *Architecture: Nineteenth and Twentieth Centuries*, p. 106.

5. Joseph-Octave Plessis, *Journal d'un Voyage en Europe 1819-20*, pp. 31-34, 38-41, 63, 76-79, and 156.

6. *Ibid.*, pp. 43-45, 156, and 256. Plessis made an interesting error when he wrote that flying buttresses were simply struts which had to be placed on the cathedrals after their construction to prevent collapse [p. 63].

7. J.-B.-A. Ferland, *Biographical Notice of Joseph-Octave Plessis*, p. 118.

8. "l'intérieur en est magnifique. Six hautes colonnes en faisceaux, de chaque côté, divisent tout le corps de l'édifice en trois nefs surmontées d'arches gothiques, formant un coup d'oeil d'autant plus imposant qu'un peintre a figuré sur le mur uni qui termine l'église derrière l'autel, une continuation de ces arches et de ces colonnes qui semblent se perdre dans le lointain et font une illusion assez forte aux étrangers non prévenus, pour leur persuader d'abord que l'autel n'est qu'à la moitié de la longueur de l'église, quoiqu'il touche réellement au fond. Le grand effet que produit cette perspective fait passer cette église pour la plus belle des Etats-Unis. Elle est encore recommandable par la grandeur de ses croisées, par l'élégance des deux jubés, l'un au-dessus de l'autre, dont les escaliers symétriques conduisent à l'orgue au-dessus de la porte d'entrée. Les bancs qui occupent la nef, y laissent trois spacieuses allées et sont couverts tout autour de tringles et accoudoirs de mahagony." (Joseph-Octave Plessis, *Journal des visites pastorales de 1815 et 1816*, pp. 161-62.) Translation in part based on John Coolidge, "Gothic Revival Churches in New England and New York," pp. 10-11.

9. Letter from Plessis to Bishop Poynter of Westminster, November 12, 1825, in *Rapport de l'Archiviste de la Province de Québec pour 1928-29*, p. 207.

10. Laval Laurent, *Québec et l'Eglise aux Etats-Unis sous Mgr. Briand et Mgr. Plessis*, pp. 130, 165.

11. *La Bibliothèque Canadienne*, IX, November 15, 1829, p. 177.

12. "Tous les architectes modernes conviennent que l'on ne peut faire usage des croisées d'ogives que dans les seules voûtes gothiques. C'est donc par une grande inadvertance, pour ne rien dire de plus, que l'on s'est permis d'en mettre dans la voûte de l'ancienne église paroissiale de Montréal. Et comme plusiers de nos prétendus architectes ne savent pas distinguer une beauté réelle d'un abus, il leur a été faute de s'imaginer que cette voûte construite dans une de nos grandes villes, était un modèle à suivre, de là toutes ces croisées d'ogive que l'on aperçoit, à notre honte et à notre confusion, dans un grand nombre de nos églises nouvellement décorées." (Jérôme Demers, "Précis d'Architecture," MS. M-765, pp. 142-43.)

13. Trudeau, "Mes Tablettes," recorded on September 14, 1825, that Roux and LeSaulnier left for Baltimore, and on June 8, 1826, the departure for Baltimore of Roux and the Reverend John Jackson Richard.

14. "Je crois que nous nous en tiendrons au Gothique et à la forme d'un quarré oblong, au moyen de quoi nous obtenons des avantages qui, suivant nous, ne sont pas balancés par ceux qui présentent la croix." (Letter from LaRocque to Thomas Baillairgé, May 8, 1824.)

15. Letter from Latrobe to Bishop Carroll of Baltimore, April 27, 1805. Copy in the Maryland Historical Society.

16. Minutes of the wardens, December 22, 1793, and minutes of the building committee, March 21, 1828, both regarding the shape and seating arrangements in the organ loft.

17. Compare *Plate* 12 with the plan of old Notre-Dame in Pierre-Louis Morin, *Le Vieux Montréal*.

18. Letter from Bourget in Marseilles to A.-J. Truteau in Montreal, June 20, 1841. Copy in Jacques Viger's "Ma Sabredache," vol. M², Archives du Séminaire de Québec.

19. On Demers, see Etienne-Théodore Paquet, *Fragments de l'Histoire Religieuse et Civile de la Paroisse de Saint-Nicolas* (Lévis, 1894), I, pp. 30 ff., and Olivier Maurault, "Un Professeur d'Architecture à Québec en 1828," *Marges d'Histoire: L'Art au Canada* (Montreal, 1929), I, pp. 93-113.

20. Letter from Demers to the building committee, April 22, 1824, repeating charges made in an earlier letter, now lost.

21. Gowans, "Notre-Dame de Montréal," p. 25.

22. *Ibid.*, p. 21. See a comparison of Notre-Dame and Saint Jacques in *Le Canadien*, V, September 8, 1824.

23. Subscription form, June 1, 1824.

24. "Fabrique Grand Livre en Rapport avec la Nouvelle Eglise 1824-1830," *passim*.

25. "[Le choeur,] qui est de la forme de ceux que l'on voit dans toutes les cathédrales d'Angleterre, mais qui n'est pas suffisamment orné pour produire son véritable effet comme à York, Lincoln, Exeter, Chichester, Windsor, etc., etc." (*La Minerve*, XXXVIII, April 28, 1866.) The writer, S. V., adds that four examples of such a choir also existed in France.

26. Morin, "Description de l'Eglise Paroissiale de la Ville de Montréal," *Mélanges Religieux*, II, November 26, 1841, p. 234.

27. The editor-in-chief of the Montreal *Standard* wrote some thirty years ago: "It is, as everyone knows, the replica of Notre-Dame in Paris." (Fred Yorston, "The Bells of Notre Dame," *The Standard*, July 6, 1935.)

28. Newton Bosworth, *Hochelaga depicta*, p. 176, on the Anglican Hochelaga Chapel.

29. Gérard Morisset, *L'Architecture en Nouvelle-France*, p. 89.

30. The widespread imitation of Notre-Dame may in part be explained as a manifestation of the ascendancy in influence of the diocese of Montreal over the diocese of Quebec. (Letter from Professor Mason Wade to the author, 1968.)

Notes to IX: Notre-Dame as a French-Canadian Church

31. Gowans, *Looking at Architecture in Canada*, pp. 41-43 and 53. The six churches were at Sainte-Famille (Ile d'Orléans), Beauport, Lauzon, Ange-Gardien, Sainte-Anne-de-Beaupré, and Château-Richer.

32. Gowans, "Thomas Baillairgé and the Tradition of Québecois Church Architecture," *Art Bulletin*, XXXIV, p. 125.

33. Morisset, *L'Architecture en Nouvelle-France*, pp. 54-56.

34. Gowans, "Thomas Baillairgé," pp. 117-37.

35. See Olivier Maurault, "La Vie de l'Eglise," *La Paroisse*, pp. 213-234, for details of this and other ceremonies. Probably the greatest ceremony of recent years in Notre-Dame was the funeral in 1967 of the French-Canadian nationalist historian Chanoine Lionel Groulx.

36. Robert Rumilly, *Henri Bourassa*, pp. 372-78, and Mason Wade, *The French Canadians 1760-1945*, pp. 579-82.

Notes to Appendix C: ART IN NOTRE-DAME

1. See the *Catalogue du Musée de Notre-Dame* (Montreal, 1961).

2. See Olivier Maurault, *La Paroisse: Histoire de l'Eglise Notre-Dame de Montréal*, p. 20, and Edward Allen Talbot, *Five Years' Residence in the Canadas*, pp. 67-8.

3. *Le Canadien*, November 27 and December 6, 1839, and J. Russell Harper, *Painting in Canada*, pp. 82-90 and plate 78.

4. Letter from Plamondon to Quiblier, June 18, 1839.

5. *Le Journal de Québec*, December 9, 1847.

6. Maurault, *La Paroisse*, pp. 87-89. The paintings are illustrated on pp. 175-76, 181-82, and 185 of the first edition of *La Paroisse*.

7. Harper, *Painting in Canada*, plate 215.

8. See *Ozias Leduc, 1864-1955, The National Gallery of Canada, Le Musée de la Province de Québec, 1955-56* (Ottawa, 1955).

9. The sculptor may have been related to or even identical with the Paul Labrosse (1697-*c.* 1760) to whom is attributed a vigorous statue of the "Virgin and Child" in the Art Gallery of Ontario. The statue is said to have come from old Notre-Dame.

10. On Quevillon, see Emile Vaillancourt, *Une Maîtrise d'Art en Canada* (Montreal, 1920), and Ramsay Traquair, *The Old Architecture of Quebec*, p. 231 *et passim*.

11. Maurault, *La Paroisse*, plate 34.

12. See pp. 68-69.

13. Ducharme claimed credit for this work in an advertisement in *La Minerve*, November 30, 1883.

14. The windows are described in detail in Maurault, *La Paroisse*, pp. 93-126, and illustrated on plates 42-52.

The great majority of unpublished manuscripts which refer to the planning, construction, and renovation of Notre-Dame are preserved in the archives of the church. The minutes of the wardens and of the building committee are bound in manuscript volumes. Letters, plans, construction estimates, and all other relevant materials are stored in boxes which are generally grouped together chronologically.

The Albion, New York, II, April 3, 1824, p. 335.

Alexander, J. E. *Transatlantic Sketches*. 2 vols. London, 1833.

Archives de la Chancellerie de l'Archevêché de Montréal. File 901.019, "Saint-Sulpice et Mgr. Lartigue"; file 901.140, "Notre-Dame — Bâtisse de l'église, 1816-1826."

"Assemblée Annuelle de la Société d'Archéologie." *Le Canada*, Montreal, XV, December 22, 1917, p. 10.

"Les Bancs de Notre-Dame depuis 1642." *La Presse*, Montreal, December 14, 1932.

La Bibliothèque Canadienne, I (June 1825) and IX (November 1829).

Bonetto, Gilles; Derome, Jacques-H.; Joyal, Laurent; and Pocevicius, Vytantas A. "Notre-Dame de Montréal." Unpublished paper, 1957. School of Architecture, McGill University, Montreal.

Borthwick, Douglas. *Historical and Graphical Gazeteer of Montreal*. Montreal, 1897.

Bosworth, Newton. *Hochelaga depicta: the early history and present state of the city and island of Montreal*. Montreal, 1839.

Bouchette, Joseph. *The British Dominions in North America*. London, 1832.

Bourassa, Napoléon. "Causerie Artistique." *La Revue Canadienne*, Montreal, n.s., IV (1867), pp. 789 ff. and 932 ff.

————. *La Minerve*, July 3, 1872.

Buckingham, James Silk. *Canada, Nova Scotia, New Brunswick and the other British Provinces in North America, with a plan of National Colonization*. London, 1843.

Canadian Magazine and Literary Repository, I (October 1823), p. 374, and III (September 1824), p. 284.

Le Canadien, Quebec, IV, October 29, 1823; V, September 8, 1824; and June 27, 1836.

Coke, E. T. *A Subaltern's Furlough*. London, 1833.

Collection Baby, Bibliothèque de l'Université de Montréal. Files H3/66 and H3/67 on Notre-Dame.

"La Décoration intérieure de l'Eglise Notre-Dame de Montréal." *Le National*, Montreal, IV, March 18, 1876.

BIBLIOGRAPHY

Dickens, Charles. *American Notes*. Greenwich, Connecticut, 1961.

Doige, Thomas. *The Montreal Directory: An Alphabetical List of the Merchants, Traders and Housekeepers Residing in Montreal, to which is Prefixed a Descriptive Sketch of the Town*. Montreal, 1819.

"L'Eglise Notre-Dame, ses Boiseries et ses Décorations en Peinture." *Le Franc-Parleur*, Montreal, V, May 21, 1875.

Fowler, Thomas. *Journal of a Tour through British America*. Aberdeen, 1832.

Gowans, Alan. "Notre-Dame de Montréal." *Journal of the Society of Architectural Historians*, XI (March 1952), pp. 20-26.

"Histoire de la Semaine." *La Revue Canadienne*, I, no. 22, May 31, 1845; no. 24, June 14, 1845.

Hontan, Baron de la. *Voyages au Canada*. Paris, 1900.

Howells, William Dean. *Their Wedding Journey*. Boston, 1872.

Huguet-Latour, Louis-Adolphe. *Annuaire de Ville-Marie*. Montreal, 1863-77.

The Irish Vindicator, Montreal, II, July 17, 1829.

Le Journal de Québec, Quebec, October 11, 1864.

MacGregor, John. *British America*. 2 vols. London, 1832.

Maurault, Olivier. *La Paroisse: Histoire de l'Eglise Notre-Dame de Montréal*. 2d ed. rev. (1st. ed., 1929.) Montreal, 1957.

La Minerve, Montreal, no. 43, July 9, 1829; no. 45, July 16, 1829.

Le Monde, Montreal, October 31, 1885.

Montreal Gazette, XXXVIII, February 4, 1830.

Montreal Gazette and Commercial Advertiser, I, September 4, 1824, and II, May 29, 1826.

Montreal Herald and Daily Commercial Gazette, March 2, 1875.

Morin, Pierre-Louis. "Description de l'Eglise Paroissiale de la Ville de Montréal ou Ville-Marie." *Mélanges Religieux*, II, November 26, 1841.

L'Opinion Publique, Montreal, V, June 25, 1874, p. 303.

Rousseau, Pierre. "Notes sur l'Eglise Notre-Dame." Unpublished manuscript *c*. 1900. Archives du Séminaire de Saint-Sulpice, Montreal.

The Scribbler, Montreal, V, June 24, 1824, p. 221

Senécal, Eusèbe. *Historical and Descriptive Notice on the Church of Notre-Dame of Montreal*. Montreal, 1880.

Sleigh, B. W. A. *Pine Forests and Hacmatack Clearings, or Travel, Life and Adventure in the British North American Provinces*. London, 1853.

Le Spectateur Canadien, Montreal, September 4, 1824.

Stone, William. *Maria Monk and the Nunnery of the Hotel Dieu, being an Account of a Visit to the Convents of Montreal*. New York, 1836. [Informative on the laying of the foundations of Notre-Dame.]

S. V. "L'Architecture en Canada: Les Eglises — Notre-Dame, Saint-Patrice et Le Gesù à Montréal." *La Minerve*, XXXVIII, no. 192, April 27, 1866; no. 193, April 28, 1866.

Symons, Scott. *Combat Journal for Place d'Armes*. Toronto, 1967.

Talbot, Edward Allen. *Five Years' Residence in the Canadas*. London, 1824.

Thoreau, Henry David. *A Yankee in Canada, with Anti-Slavery and Reform Papers*. Boston, 1866.

Trudeau, Romuald. "Mes Tablettes." Unpublished manuscript, 1823-41. Bibliothèque Nationale, Annexe Aegidieux Fauteux, Montreal. Typed copy in the Bibliothèque de la Ville de Montréal.

Vignot, Pierre. *Carême de Montréal*. Paris, 1907.

Warburton, Eliot. *Hochelaga: or, England in the New World*. 2 vols. New York, 1846.

Willis, N. P. *Canadian Scenery*. Illustrated by W. H. Bartlett. 2 vols. London, 1842.

Addison, Agnes. *Romanticism and the Gothic Revival*. New York, 1938.

Alexander, Robert L. "Architecture and Aristocracy: The Cosmopolitan Style of Latrobe and Godefroy." *Maryland Historical Magazine*, LVI (September 1961), pp. 229-43.

"The Architectural Review Gothic Number." *Architectural Review*, 98 (December 1945), pp. 149-80.

Banham, Reyner. "Convenient Benches and Handy Hooks: Functional Considerations in the Criticism of the Art of Architecture." In *The History, Theory and Criticism of Architecture*. Edited by Marcus Whiffen. Cambridge, Massachusetts, 1965.

Bédard, Pierre-H. *Lettre à M. Chaboillez . . . Relativement à ses questions sur le gouvernement ecclésiastique du district de Montréal*. Montreal, 1823.

Bédard, T.-P. *Histoire de Cinquante Ans: 1791-1841*. Quebec, 1869.

Benjamin, Asher. *The American Builder's Companion*. 3d. ed. rev. Boston, 1816.

Berthelot, Hector. *Montréal: Le Bon Vieux Temps*. Edited by E.-Z. Massicotte. 2 vols. Montreal, 1916.

Biddle, Owen. *The Young Carpenter's Assistant*. Philadelphia, 1805.

Blondel, Jacques-François. *Architecture Française*. Paris, 1752.

Brown, Thomas Storrow. "Montreal in 1818." *New Dominion Monthly*, March 30, 1870, pp. 19-30.

Burke, Edmund. *A Philosophical Inquiry into the Origin of Our Ideas of the Sublime and Beautiful*. New York, 1829.

Carthy, Mary Peter. *Old St. Patrick's*. New York, 1947.

The Centenary of the Bank of Montreal 1817-1917. Montreal, 1917.

Chaboillez, Augustin. *Questions sur le Gouvernement Ecclésiastique du District de Montréal*. Montreal, 1823.

"The Churches of New York." *Putnam's Monthly*, II (1853), pp. 234-54.

Clark, Kenneth. *The Gothic Revival: An Essay in the History of Taste*. 3d. ed. London, 1962.

Colvin, H. M. "Gothic Survival and Gothic Revival." *Architectural Review*, CIII (March 1958), pp. 91-98.

Condit, Carl W. *American Building Art: The Nineteenth Century*. New York, 1960.

Considérations sur les biens du Séminaire de Montréal. Montreal, n.d. [1824?]

Consultation de douze des plus célèbres avocats de Paris, touchant les droits de propriété du Séminaire de Montréal en Canada. Paris, 1819.

Coolidge, John. "Gothic Revival Churches in New England and New York." Unpublished honours thesis, Harvard University, 1935. Harvard College Library, Cambridge, Massachusetts; copy in Avery Architectural Library, New York.

Coyle, Mary Ann. "Victor Bourgeau, Architect: A Biographical Sketch." Unpublished manuscript, 1960. School of Architecture, McGill University, Montreal.

Craig, Maurice. *Dublin 1660-1860*. London, 1952.

Daveluy, Marie-Claire. *La Société de Notre-Dame de Montréal 1639-1663*. Montreal, 1965.

Demers, Jérôme. "Précis d'Architecture." Unpublished manuscript, c. 1826-28. Archives du Séminaire de Québec; photostat copy in the School of Architecture, McGill University.

De Mille, George E. *St. Thomas Church in the City and County of New York 1823-1954*. Austin, Texas, 1958.

Denison, Merrill. *History of the Bank of Montreal*. 2 vols. Montreal, 1967.

De Volpi, Charles and Winkworth, Peter. *Montréal: Recueil Iconographique: A Pictorial Record*. 2 vols. Montreal, 1963.

Dollier de Casson, François. *A History of Montreal 1640-1672*. Edited and translated by Ralph Flenley. London, 1928.

BIBLIOGRAPHY

Dupin, André-Marie-J.-J. *Opinion of Mr. Dupin, Advocate, of the Royal Court of Paris, on the Rights of the Seminary of Montreal, in Canada.* Montreal, 1840.

Faillon, Etienne-Michel. *Histoire de la Colonie Française en Canada.* 3 vols. Villemarie (Montreal), 1865-66.

Ferland, J-B.-A. *Biographical Notice of Joseph-Octave Plessis, Bishop of Quebec.* Translated by T. B. French. Quebec, 1864.

——. *Mgr. Joseph-Octave Plessis.* Quebec, 1878.

Frankl, Paul. *The Gothic: Literary Sources and Interpretations through Eight Centuries.* Princeton, New Jersey, 1960.

Garneau, François-Xavier. *Histoire du Canada.* 8th. ed., annotated. Montreal, 1945.

Garvan, Anthony. "The Protestant Plain Style before 1630." *Journal of the Society of Architectural Historians,* IX (October 1950), pp. 4-13.

Gauthier, Henri. *Sulpitiana.* Montreal, 1926.

Gibbs, James. *A Book of Architecture, Containing Designs of Buildings and Ornaments.* London, 1728.

Gowans, Alan. *Church Architecture in New France.* Toronto, 1955.

——. *Looking at Architecture in Canada.* Toronto, 1958. (2d ed. rev., *Building Canada,* Toronto, 1966.)

——. "Thomas Baillairgé and the Tradition of Québecois Church Architecture." *Art Bulletin,* XXXIV (1952), pp. 117-37.

——. "The Baroque Revival in Québec." *Journal of the Society of Architectural Historians,* XIV (October 1955), pp. 8-14.

Guinness, Desmond. *Portrait of Dublin.* London, 1967.

Guy, Louis and Viger, Jacques. "Dénombrement du Comté de Montréal fait en 1825 par Louis Guy et Jacques Viger." Unpublished manuscript, 1825. Microfilm copy, Salle Gagnon, Bibliothèque de la Ville de Montréal.

Hall, Margery A. "History of St. Paul's Church, Fairfax Parish, Alexandria, Virginia." Mimeographed manuscript, 1932. Archives of St. Paul's Church, Alexandria.

Harper, J. Russell. *Painting in Canada.* Toronto, 1966.

—— and Triggs, Stanley. *Portrait of a Period: A Collection of Notman Photographs 1856 to 1915.* Montreal, 1967.

Hitchcock, Henry-Russell. *Architecture: Nineteenth and Twentieth Centuries.* Baltimore, 1958.

Hopkins, John Henry. *Essay on Gothic Architecture . . . for the use of the Clergy.* Burlington, Vermont, 1836.

Hubbard, Robert. "Canadian Gothic." *Architectural Review,* CXVI (August 1954), pp. 102-8.

Langley, Batty. *Gothic Architecture, Improved by Rules and Proportions.* London, 1742.

LaRocque, François-Antoine. "The Missouri Journal 1804-05." In L.-R. Masson, *Les Bourgeois de la Compagnie du Nord-Ouest.* Quebec, 1889.

——. *Journal of Larocque from the Assiniboine to the Yellowstone, 1805.* Edited by L. J. Burpee. Ottawa, 1910.

Latrobe, Benjamin Henry. Manuscript copies of his letters in the Maryland Historical Society, Baltimore (1804-17), and in the Manuscripts Division, Library of Congress, Washington (1805-17, with reference to the Capitol).

Laurent, Laval. *Québec et l'Eglise aux Etats-Unis sous Mgr. Briand et Mgr. Plessis.* Washington, D.C., 1945.

Maurault, Olivier. "Dollier de Casson." *Revue Trimestrielle Canadienne,* IV (1919), pp. 361-70.

——. *Saint-Jacques de Montréal.* Montreal, 1923.

McLean, Eric. *The Living Past of Montreal.* Montreal, 1964.

Milner, John. *Treatise on the Ecclesiastical Architecture of England.* London, 1811.

Morin, Pierre-Louis. *Le Vieux Montréal.* Montreal, 1884.

Morisset, Gérard. *L'Architecture en Nouvelle-France.* Quebec, 1949.

O'Donnell, James. "Last Will and Testament of James O'Donnell." November 14, 1829 Archives Judiciaires, Palais de Justice, Montreal.

Ouellet, Fernand. *Histoire Economique et Sociale du Québec 1760-1850*. Montreal, 1966.

Pilcher, Donald. *The Regency Style 1800 to 1830*. London, 1947.

Plessis, Joseph-Octave. *Journal des visites pastorales de 1815 et 1816 par Monseigneur Joseph-Octave Plessis, évêque de Québec*. Edited by Henri Têtu. Quebec, 1903.

———. *Journal d'un Voyage en Europe 1819-1820*. Edited by Henri Têtu. Quebec, 1903.

———. "Inventaire de la correspondence de Mgr. J.-O. Plessis." *Rapport de l'Archiviste de la Province de Québec pour 1928-29* (Quebec, 1930), pp. 87-208, and *Rapport de l'Archiviste pour 1932-33* (Quebec, 1933), pp. 1-244.

Port, M. H. *Six Hundred New Churches: A Study of the Church Building Commission, 1818-1856, and Its Church Building Activities*. London, 1961.

Pouliot, Léon. "Il y a cent ans: le démembrement de la paroisse Notre-Dame." *Revue d'Histoire de l'Amérique Française*, XIX (1965), pp. 350-83.

"Records of the American Academy of the Fine Arts." Manuscript volume, n.d. Library of The New-York Historical Society, New York.

Rickman, Thomas. *An Attempt to Discriminate Styles of Architecture in England*. London, 1817.

Ritchie, Thomas. *Canada Builds: 1867-1967*. Toronto, 1967.

Rumilly, Robert. *Henri Bourassa*. Montreal, 1953.

Rusk, William Sener. "Godefroy and Saint Mary's Chapel, Baltimore." *Liturgical Arts*, II (1934), pp. 141-45.

Sandham, Alfred. *Montreal and Its Fortifications*. Montreal, 1874.

S. N. *The Jesuit*, Boston, I (1830). [Death of James O'Donnell.]

Stanton, Phoebe B. *An Episode in Taste: The Gothic Revival and American Church Architecture*. Baltimore, 1968. [Not available to the author for consultation.]

Summerson, John. *Georgian London*. Baltimore, 1962.

———. *Architecture in Britain 1530 to 1830*. Baltimore, 1954.

Têtu, Henri and Gagnon, C.-O., eds. *Mandements, Lettres Pastorales et Circulaires des Evêques de Québec*. Quebec, 1888.

Traquair, Ramsay. *The Old Architecture of Quebec*. Toronto, 1947.

Le Troisième Centenaire de Saint-Sulpice. Montreal, 1941.

Viger, Jacques. "Ma Sabredache" and "Album de Jacques Viger." Manuscripts written *c.* 1820-40. Archives du Séminaire de Québec, Quebec.

Wade, Mason. *The French Canadians 1760-1945*. Toronto, 1955.

Whiffen, Marcus. *Stuart and Georgian Churches*. London, 1947.

———. "The Progeny of St. Martin in the Fields." *Architectural Review*, C (July 1946), pp. 3-6.

White, James F. *The Cambridge Movement: The Ecclesiologists and the Gothic Revival*. Cambridge, England, 1962.

Buildings outside Montreal are listed by city; buildings in Montreal have separate entries.

National, Le (Montreal), 46, 77
New York: buildings by O'Donnell, 25-27, 30; St. Patrick's Old Cathedral, 26, 39, 74; St. Thomas Church, 34, 39; St. Paul's Chapel, 35; St. Patrick's Cathedral, 59
Notre-Dame de Montréal
first and second churches, 6
third church: founded, 2; described, 8; obsolete, 9; status of, 10; destroyed, 52; Gothic elements in, 75
fourth (existing) church: facade of, 2, 40, 49; interior of, as a theatre, 3, 62, 70; and Georgian style, 3, 35; subdivision of the parish, 15, 65; financing of, 16, 19, 49, 52, 78; and patrons, 18; as symbol of French Canada, 19, 73; O'Donnell's first design of, 29-31, Pl. 9; as pioneer Gothic Revival design in Canada, 30, 73; O'Donnell's second design of, 31-42; structural system of, 33, 35, 47-49, 59; and St. Thomas, New York, 34; optical illusions in, 34, 36; and third church of Notre-Dame, 36, 76; and relation to city of Montreal, 37, 42; and St. Paul's, Alexandria, 38; towers of, 39, 60; flanks of, 41; workers on, 43; construction of, 43-49 *passim*; materials for, 44, 47, 52; roof of, 47; renovation of 1961, 48-49; decoration of, 49-51, 91-94; opened, 51; bells of, 60; renovation of 1872, 65-71 *passim*; provincial copies of, 67, 75, 79; reredos of, 68-69; sacristy of, 70; Chapelle du Sacré-Coeur, 71; critical appraisal of, 77-82 *passim*
Notre-Dame Street, Montreal, 2, 8, 32

O'Donnell, James, 23-28; and the Gothic Revival, 24, 76; first and second designs for Notre-Dame, 29-42; and Latrobe, 38; and Josiah Brady, 39; and modular conception of the facade, 40; on Canadian workmen, 43; on estimate of materials, 47; reputation in Canada, 53; other works in Montreal, 54-55; on life in New York, 56; on science, 56; character of, 56; death of, 58; letter to LaRocque, 83-86
Olier, Jean-Jacques, 5-6
Ostell, John, 49, 55, 60

Pain, George and Richard, 38
Papineau family, 11-12, 55
Paris: Seminary of Saint-Sulpice, 6; church of Saint-Sulpice, 19, 36, 39, 50; Sainte-Chapelle, 68; Notre-Dame Cathedral, 74, 78
Peterborough Cathedral, 38
Pienovi, Angelo, 49, 66, 92
Place d'Armes, Montreal, 1, 2, 8, 9, 32, 42
Plamondon, Antoine, 92
Plessis, Joseph-Octave, 10-11, 13, 18, 52, 74
Proctor, John, 20, 33
Pugin, Augustus Charles, 51

Quebec province: architecture in, 2, 19, 67, 71, 77, 80; nationalism in, 18, 78, 81

Redpath, John, 43, 44
Renwick, James, Sr., 27
Revue Canadienne, La (Montreal), 60
Rickman, Thomas, 50
Rochester, New York: First Presbyterian Church, 26-27, 30
Rollin, Paul, 49, 51, 93
Rousseau, Pierre, 57-58
Rousselot, Benjamin-Victor, 65-66, 68, 78

Saint-Barthélémi, Quebec, parish church, 67, 79-80, Pl. 52

Saint-Jacques Cathedral, Montreal, 13, 19, 59, 66, 79, 80, 107 n.26

Saint-Joseph Street, Montreal (now Saint-Sulpice), 2, 6, 8, 41

Saint-Pierre-Apôtre Church, Montreal, 66

Saint-Sulpice, order of (Sulpicians): Seminary building, 5; and founding of Montreal, 5-6; and control over Montreal, 7-9; and church of Notre-Dame, 8, 16, 61, 66, 75; and priests from revolutionary France, 9, 75; and Bishop Plessis, 10-13; criticism of, 12

Saint-Sulpice Street, Montreal. *See* Saint-Joseph Street

Sainte-Anne-de-la-Pérade, parish church of, 79, Pl. 51

Sawyer, August, 66

Seigniorial system, 7

Sleigh, B. W. A., 59

Strickland, William, 31, 39

Thoreau, Henry David, 61

Traquair, Ramsay, 73

Trudeau, Romuald, 75

Vanderlyn, John, 20-21

Viger family, 11-13, 55

Viger, Jacques, 12

Wade, Mason, 111 n.30

Wardens of the church of Notre-Dame, 51, 52, 66; building a new church, 9, 15-16, 29, 77; opposition to Lartigue, 11, 13

Willcocks, Lewis, 20, 48, 75

Plates

1. Notre-Dame seen from the air.

2. Montreal in 1815. *See page 1.*

3. Old Notre-Dame in 1826. *See pages 9, 80.*

4. Place d'Armes in 1830. *See page 2.*

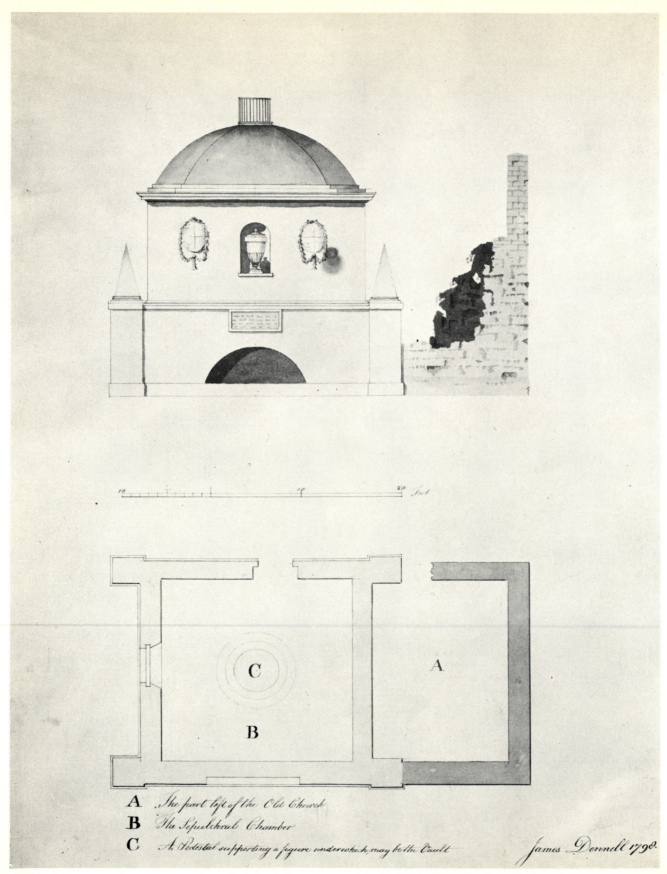

A The part left of the Old Church
B The Sepulchral Chamber
C A Pedestal supporting a figure under which may be the Vault

James Donnell 1798

5. James O'Donnell, plan and elevation of a mausoleum, 1798. *See page 24.*

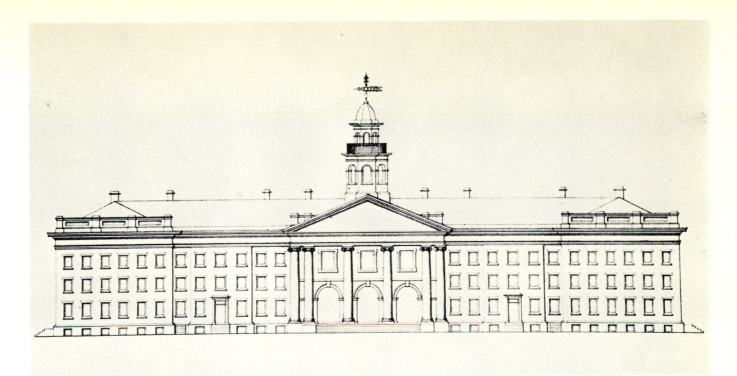

6. James O'Donnell, elevation for Columbia College, New York, 1817. *See page 25.*

7. Christ Church, New York, 1823. James O'Donnell, architect. *See page 26.*

8.   The First Presbyterian Church, Rochester, 1824.
James O'Donnell, architect. *See page 26.*

9. Reconstruction of O'Donnell's first design for Notre-Dame, 1823. *See page 30.*

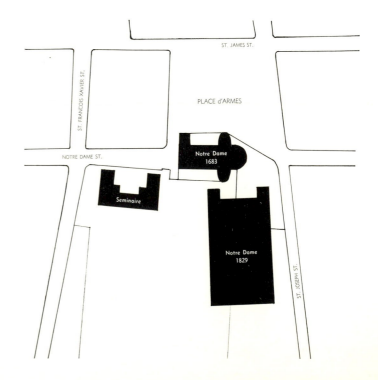

10. Site plan of Notre-Dame. *See page 32.*

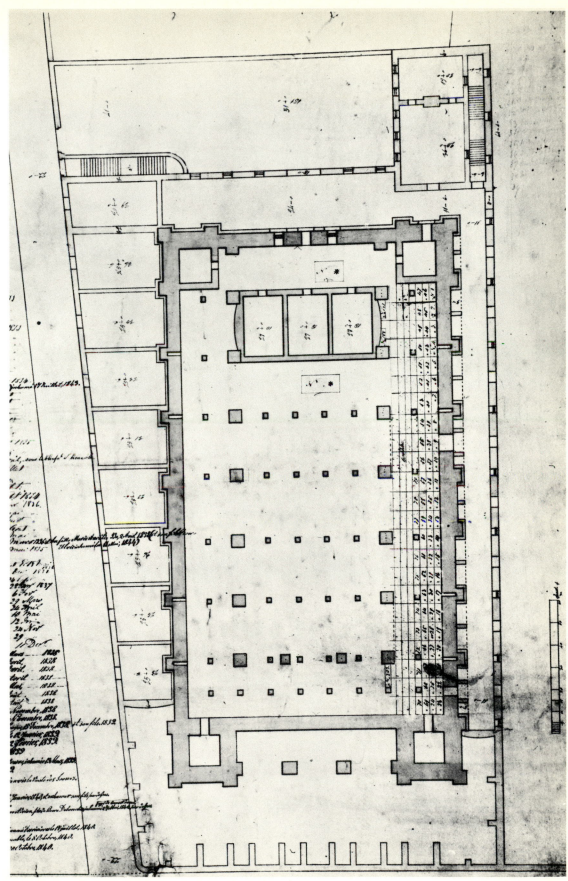

11. James O'Donnell, plan of the crypt. *See page 32.*

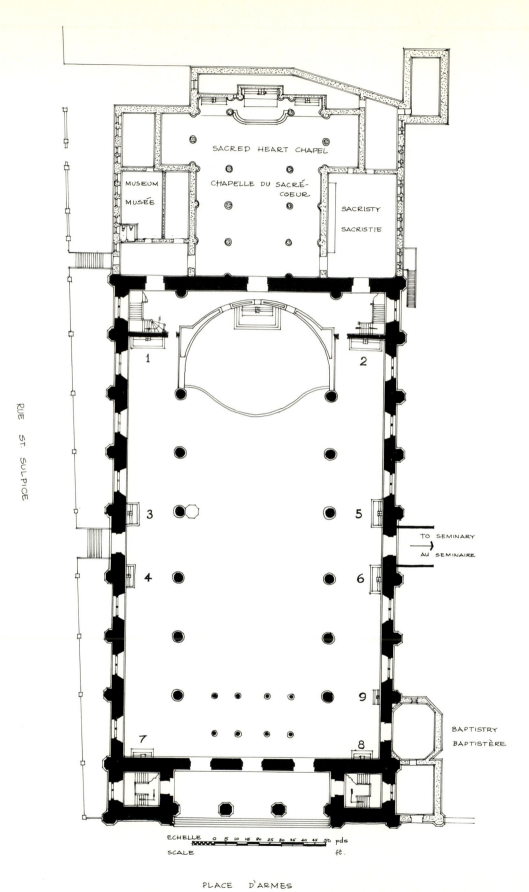

SACRED HEART CHAPEL

CHAPELLE DU SACRÉ-
COEUR

MUSEUM

MUSÉE

SACRISTY

SACRISTIE

RUE ST. SULPICE

1

2

3

5

TO SEMINARY

AU SEMINAIRE

4

6

9

BAPTISTRY

BAPTISTÈRE

7

8

ECHELLE   0 5 10 15 20 25 30 35 40 45 50 pds

SCALE   ft.

PLACE D'ARMES

12. Ground plan of Notre-Dame with later additions. *See page 33.*

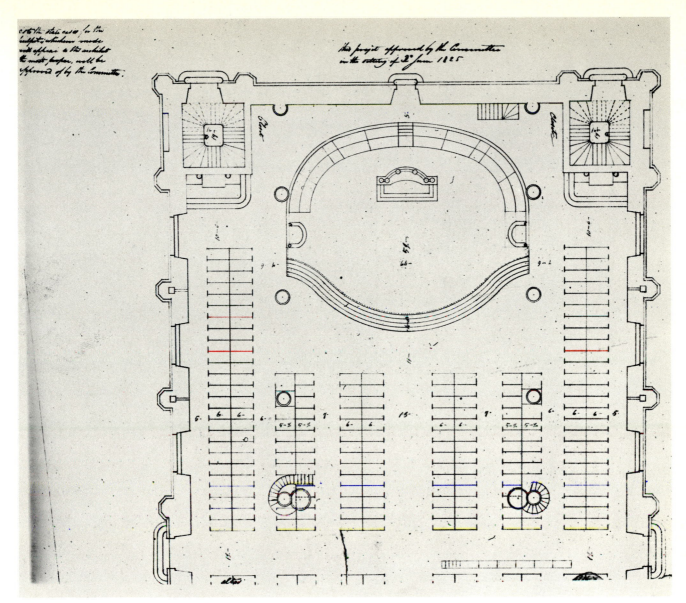

13. James O'Donnell, proposed plan of the sanctuary, 1825. *See page 36.*

14. Interior of Notre-Dame looking east, 1829. *See page 51.*

15. Interior of Notre-Dame looking west, 1829.

16. Interior of Notre-Dame, *c.* 1838. *See page 62.*

17. Interior of Notre-Dame, 1860. *See page 60.*

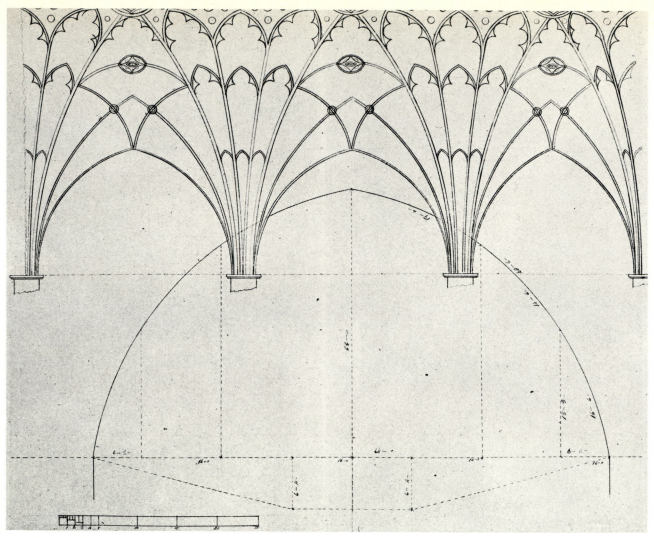

18. James O'Donnell, detail of the ceiling elevation. *See page 35.*

19. James O'Donnell, plan of the ceiling. *See page 36*.

20. St. Martin's-in-the-Fields, London, 1726. James Gibbs, architect. *See page 35.*

21. Interior of Notre-Dame.

22. The Chapel Royal, Dublin, 1812. Francis Johnston, architect. *See pages 24, 36.*

23. Exterior of Notre-Dame.

24. Modular system of the facade. *See page 40.*

THE CATHOLIC CHURCH MONTREAL.

25. Exterior of Notre-Dame in 1834 (towers and terrace added by the artist).

26. Notre-Dame and the Séminaire de Saint-Sulpice.

27. St. Paul's, Alexandria, Virginia, 1818. Benjamin Henry Latrobe, architect. (Photograph reversed.) *See page 38.*

28. Exterior of Notre-Dame, *c.* 1838.

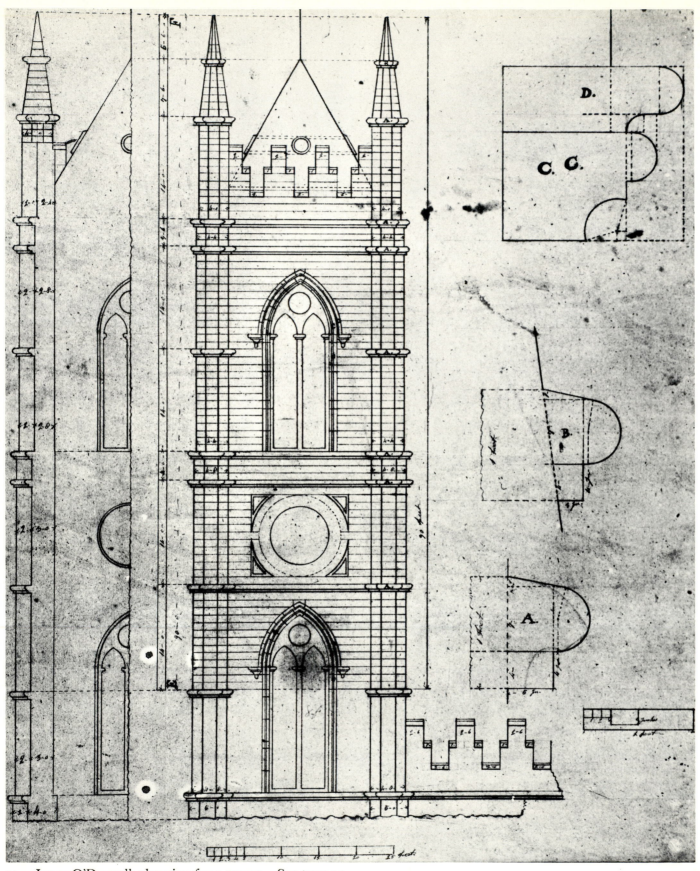

29. James O'Donnell, elevation for a tower. *See page 39.*

30. Northern flank of Notre-Dame. *See page 31.*

31.   Southern flank of Notre-Dame in 1829 (towers added by the artist).

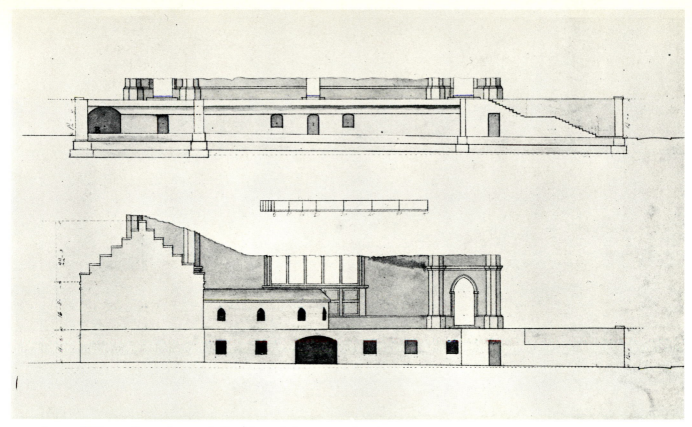

32.   James O'Donnell, section and elevation of the east end.   *See page 32.*

33. Notre-Dame seen from the suburbs of Montreal in 1838. *See page 42.*

34. Notre-Dame seen from the St. Lawrence River in 1842.

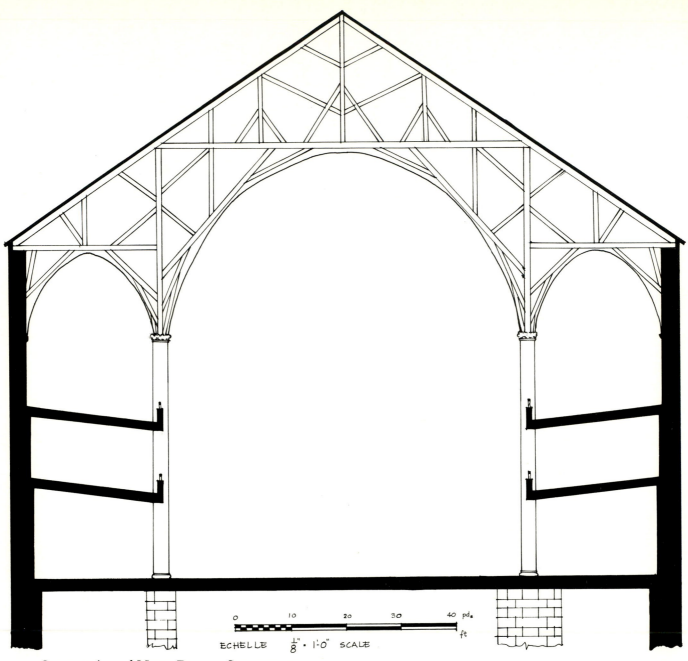

ECHELLE ⅛" · 1'-0" SCALE

35. Cross-section of Notre-Dame. *See page* 47.

36. Scale model of Notre-Dame. *See page 35.*

37. The *forêt* of Notre-Dame. *See page* 47.

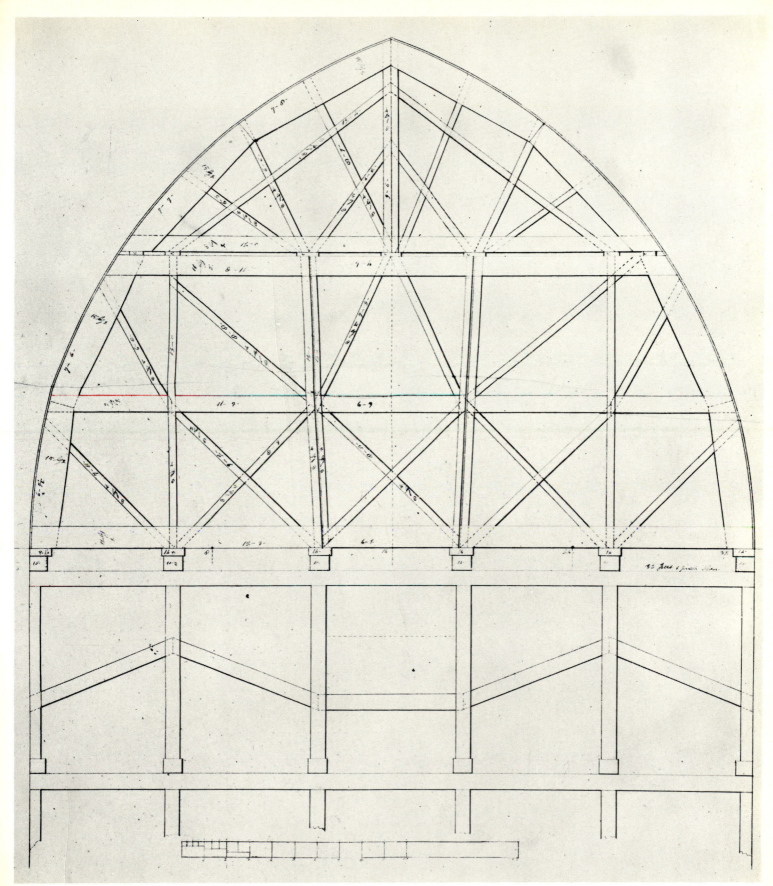

38. James O'Donnell, centering for the east window. *See page 48.*

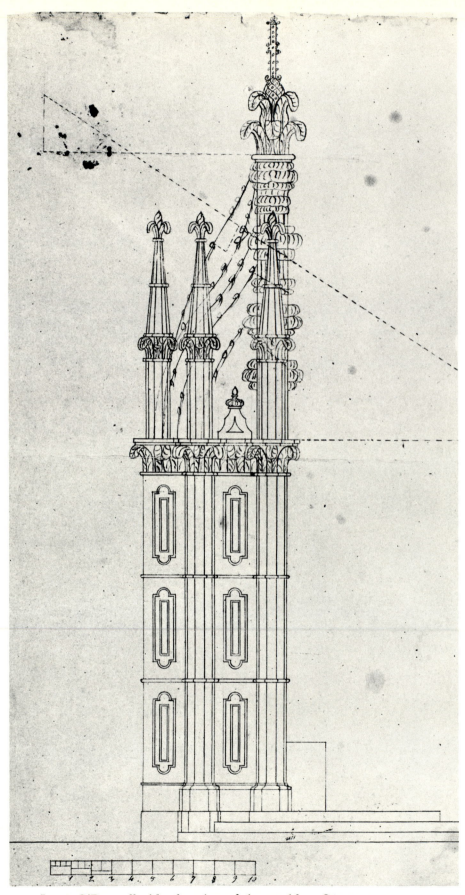

39. James O'Donnell, side elevation of the retable. *See page 49.*

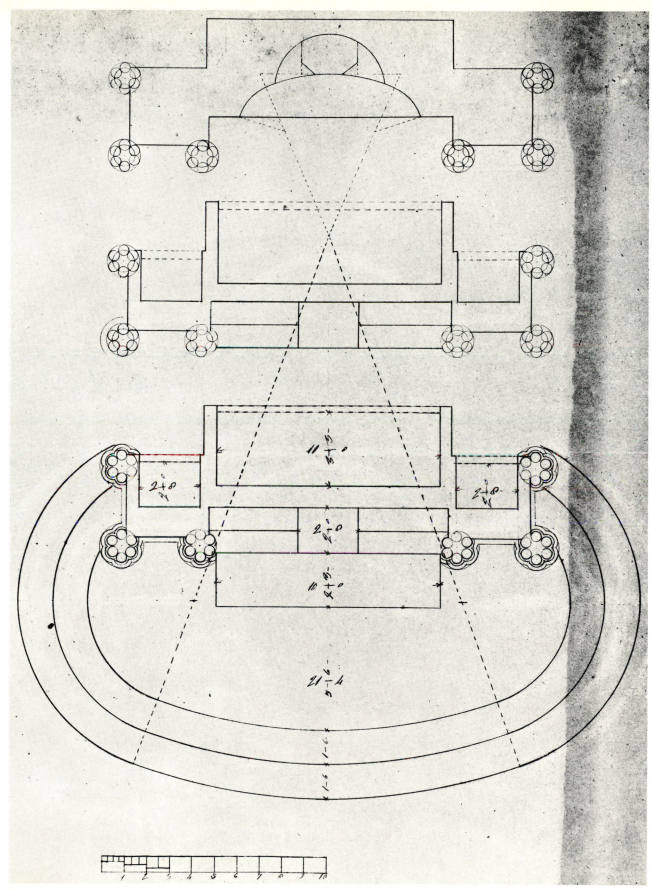

40. James O'Donnell, plan of the retable.

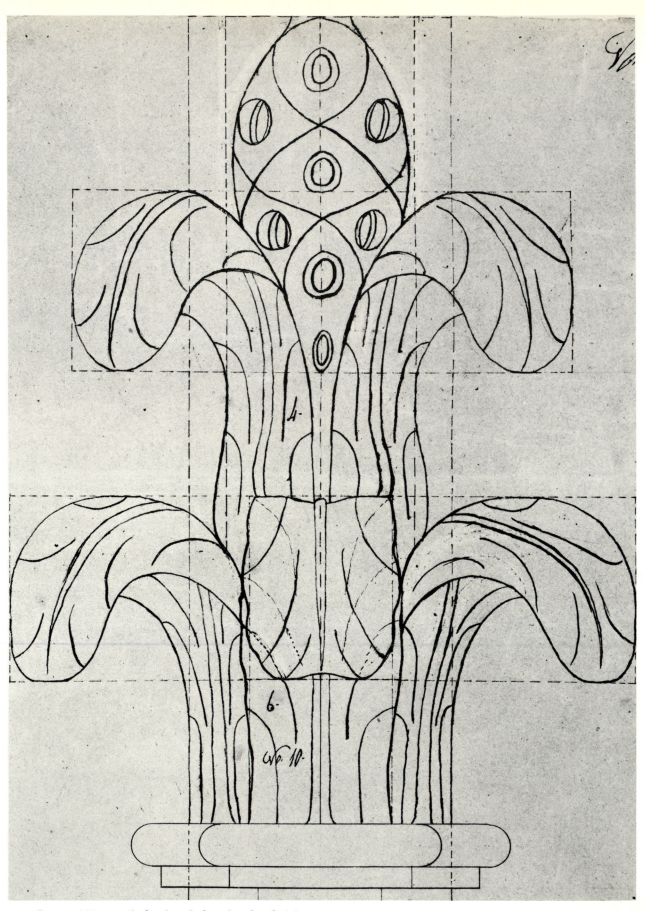

41. James O'Donnell, freehand sketch of a finial.

42. The sanctuary of Notre-Dame in 1871 (Ash Wednesday). *See page 50.*

43.   Interior of Notre-Dame in 1873 (the funeral of Sir Georges-Etienne Cartier).   *See page 81.*

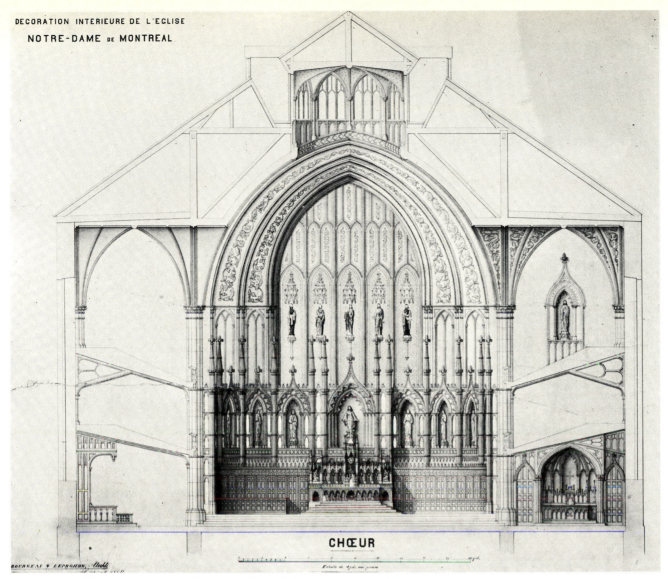

CHŒUR

44. Victor Bourgeau, proposed renovation of the sanctuary, 1869. *See page* 67.

45. Sanctuary of Notre-Dame. *See page 68.*

46. Pulpit and sanctuary of Notre-Dame.

47.   Interior of Notre-Dame looking west.

48. The pulpit of Notre-Dame. *See page 70.*

49. Chapelle du Sacré-Coeur in Notre-Dame. *See page 71.*

50. A stained glass window in Notre-Dame, representing the construction in 1829, the Eucharistic Congress of 1910, and the consecration in 1929. *See page 94.*

51. Parish church of Sainte-Anne-de-la-Pérade, Quebec, 1869. Casimir Coursol, architect. *See page 79.*

52. Parish church of Saint-Barthélémi, Quebec, 1868. Victor Bourgeau, architect. *See page 80.*

53. American Presbyterian Church, Montreal, 1826. James O'Donnell, architect. *See page 54.*

54. British and Canadian School, Montreal, 1827. James O'Donnell, architect. *See page 55.*